Bearing Up

Other titles by Randell Jones

Scoundrels, Rogues, and Heroes of the Old North State, 2004 & 2007
    by Dr. H.G. Jones, edited by Randell Jones & Caitlin Jones

In the Footsteps of Daniel Boone, 2005
    with *On the Trail of Daniel Boone* (companion DVD), 2005

In the Footsteps of Davy Crockett, 2006

Before They Were Heroes at King's Mountain, 2011

A Guide to the Overmountain Victory National Historic Trail, 2011,
    second edition, 2016

Trailing Daniel Boone, DAR marking Daniel Boone's Trail, 1912-1915,
    2012

The Daniel Boone Wagon Train—a journey through The Sixties, 2013

Interactive, Online Tour of the Overmountain Victory NH Trail, 2014
    (link from www.danielboonefootsteps.com)

Interactive, Online Tour of Daniel Boone's Trail, 2015
    (link from www.danielboonefootsteps.com)

The American Spirit, 1780, 2016 (free YouTube video)
    (link from www.danielboonefootsteps.com)

From Time to Time in North Carolina, 2017

Thumped by History, 2017

Available through Daniel Boone Footsteps
www.danielboonefootsteps.com
1959 N. Peace Haven Rd., #105
Winston-Salem, NC 27106

Bearing Up

Randell Jones. editor

Daniel Boone Footsteps
Winston-Salem, North Carolina

Daniel Boone Footsteps
1959 N. Peace Haven Rd., #105
Winston-Salem, NC 27106

www.danielboonefootsteps.com
DBooneFootsteps@gmail.com

From Dreams to Realities by William H. McCann, Jr.
"Letter: April 11, 1962" was first published in **Kaleidoscope**,
    Winter/Spring Online 2017, Issue 74, page 77.
"Dreamers" was first published in **Kaleidoscope**,
    Summer/Fall Online 2017, Issue 75, page 31.

Can You Move It?, **The Day I Was Fired**, and **Show-and-Tell Goddess**, by Diane Pascoe were first published in
Life Isn't Perfect but My Lipstick Is, 2017

The best way out is always through.
- Robert Frost

Preface

This book grew from an interest in helping celebrate in 2019 the 250th anniversary of an important event in American history: Daniel Boone's first passage through the Cumberland Gap into Kentucky in spring 1769. Cumberland Gap is America's first "gateway to the west" and the portal through which a quarter-million immigrants passed from 1775 to 1810 to populate an expanding American frontier.

As part of this celebration effort, we chose to engage modern Americans in writing about experiences in their lives which resonate with themes associated with Boone's experiences during his first excursion into Kentucky: exploration, discovery, and adventure. We created the Personal Essay Publishing Project.

To test the publishing concept, we launched a pilot project in November 2017 by issuing a Call for Essays concerning an event in the life of Daniel Boone in 1767/1768—his wintering over after being trapped by an early snow storm in the mountains of eastern Kentucky. This book is the result of that first Call for Essays. The success of this pilot project encourages us to issue our planned Call for Essays in summer 2018 for helping celebrate during 2019 the 250th anniversary of Boone's Cumberland Gap passage.

We thank first and foremost the several dozen writers in Kentucky and North Carolina who responded to the Call for Essays by submitting such interesting, thoughtful, and well-crafted essays on the themes of "making do, bearing up, and overcoming adversity."

We also thank the following organizations who helped connect our Call for Essays with communities of writers in two states:

Winston-Salem Writers, Inc.

North Carolina Writers Network, Inc.

Carnegie Center for Literacy and Learning
    (Lexington, KY)

Charlotte Writers Club

Louisville Literary Arts

Fort Boonesborough State Park

Capitol City Writers Roundtable (Frankfort, KY)

Bell County Public Library (KY)

Owensboro Writers' Group (KY)

Grant County Writers' Group (KY)

Eagle Creek Writers' Group (Lexington, KY)

Writers Group of the Triad (Greensboro, NC)

Women Who Write (KY)

Charlotte Center for Literary Arts

And, we especially thank "Artist of the American Frontier" David Wright for the kind use of his image, "A Sound in the Stillness," as our cover art. (www.DavidWrightArt.com) •

Contents

Contents

Contents

Introduction

Everybody loves a good story; and, everybody has a story to tell. Some folks just need the right opportunity and perhaps a little encouragement to share a tale they want to tell. That is the mission of the Personal Essay Publishing Project, a chance for both new and experienced writers to craft a story from their own lives and then to see their creative efforts around a common theme shared in print in a collective anthology.

The project was born out of a sincere desire to help modern Americans connect with the stories of those who came before us, those who helped create the America of which we find ourselves its current stewards. History is not often a happy story, and our collective history is rich with experiences from which we can learn how better to live our lives into our collective future.

Daniel Boone

One of the icons of America's early years is Daniel Boone. He is America's pioneer hero whose remarkable life spanned 86 years from colonial times before the American Revolution into the rise of Andrew Jackson. During his life, Boone's footsteps passed through what today is divided into 11 states, spanning from Pennsylvania to Missouri, and from the Great Lakes to Florida swamps. (See *In the Footsteps of Daniel Boone* by Randell Jones.)

Next year, 2019, is the 250th anniversary of Daniel Boone's first excursion through the Cumberland Gap into Kentucky in spring 1769. He hunted there for two years ranging across the vast interior of the Bluegrass State before returning home to the upper Yadkin River valley of North Carolina. Six years later, he would mark Boone Trace in March 1775 along which some of the earliest immigrants into Kentucky would pass during the following 20 years.

But there is another story—a lesser known story—which occurred the year before 1769 and begs for acknowledgement and appreciation. This is the story which gave rise to the Personal Essay Publishing Project and the publishing of *Bearing Up.*

Snowbound in the Wilderness

After the fall harvest in 1767, Daniel Boone left his Wilkes County home on Beaver Creek in North Carolina for a winter hunt. Boone and his companion, William Hill, passed through the Appalachian Mountains along the Russell Fork of the Big Sandy River. That water gap lies today in Breaks Interstate Park, straddling the border between Virginia and Kentucky near Elkhorn City, Kentucky. The hunters were caught in the wilderness by an early and heavy snow storm. The snow was too deep for them to walk out; they had to winter-over.

The men's supplies ran low, especially shot and powder for their rifles. Rather than exhaust themselves and squander their precious ammunition by chasing scarce game through the deep snow, they built a makeshift shelter at a salt spring near today's David, Kentucky. They conserved their resources by waiting to shoot the wild game which came their way seeking the salt. Boone and Hill survived the winter through their woodsman skills, by making do. Enduring the monotony of being snow-bound, they kept their spirits high, and throughout their ordeal their resolve to overcome their adverse circumstances never waned. After surviving a long, harsh winter, the men returned home in the spring of 1768, having had quite an adventure and delighting their worried families with their long-awaited return.

Telling One's Own Story

To enable writers to connect with the spirit of Daniel Boone in facing this wilderness challenge, we issued a Call for Essays during the winter of 2017/2018. In the spirit of finding one-self in a challenging circumstance and persevering by making do, we invited writers to craft a personal essay about some experience of their own lives in which they made do, kept their spirits high, or their resolve strong. Or perhaps their experience did not end so positively. In any case, we invited writers to share their stories in 750-800 words in a personal essay. We invited only North Carolina and Kentucky writers to participate.

Bearing Up

We were gratified by the response to our Call for Essays, and we are grateful to all who invested time and energy into craft-ing personal essays for possible inclusion in this anthology. We chose essays to include based on the quality of the writing and the resonance of the personal experiences shared with the theme of the Call for Essays: making do, bearing up, and overcoming adversity.

The essays presented here are a testament that good storytelling is alive and well. Some will make you wince, some cry, some cheer, and some laugh out loud. All are shared in the hope that your own stories of bearing up during challenging times will come to your mind and that you might write them and share them in your own circle of friends and family.

Remember, everybody loves a good story. •

In May 1948, Daniel Boone Troop 143 of the
Boy Scouts of America in Floyd County, Kentucky,
erected a monument built of river stone and including
a plaque which commemorates the wintering-over of
Daniel Boone at the salt springs in 1767/1768.

The Gift

by Lisa Miracle Ballard

L et me tell you a little story. That's a famous line in my family.

My dad, born of a deep lineage of storytellers from the "hollers" of southeastern Kentucky, always started his "life lessons" this way. It's how I know my history, my ancestors and my heritage. It was the colorful depiction of their hard-fought life in a land that fought back; generations of miners, soldiers, healers, and teachers that helped me know who I am. Our shared journey of struggle sowed seeds of strength into me and took root. In one of my darkest hours I reached back and took hold of my heritage to pull myself out of a personal catastrophe.

In my senior year of college, I was caught in the middle of a 22-car pileup in a whiteout. I could not know then that the voice of a grandmother from ages past would restore me to life. But she did. And it was my dad, the story teller, who gave life to her voice to pass life back to me.

On February 24th, 1990, I was heading south on I-75, leaving school and three jobs in my rearview. Going home! What sweet words! Lost in my thoughts of the future I had worked so hard for, I found myself going too fast. I moved over to the driving lane and got behind a truck going too slow.

Oh come on! I thought as I slowed down. And **that** was my last thought.

Without warning, everything disappeared. The world went white! In a single blink there was no sight, no sound, just white.

Time splintered. I was tumbling through space. Metallic screams broke the silence amidst my blindness. Crushing, grinding sounds pierced through my deafness. And I endured impact with distant collisions rumbling. Pain, panic, chaos. Consciousness came and went. I awoke in my parents' home. But all I could hold in my mind was that singular moment of blindness behind the wheel.

It would be a long recovery.

In the next weeks I fell into despair. I had to face reality, that life as I knew it was over. I would walk again, eventually. I would see again. I would talk again. But, it would not be the life I had known. The goals that had seemed just within my reach were forever gone.

Despair darkened my every moment. Pain overwhelmed me. I didn't know how to go on. My mom, ever-wise, told my dad, "She's given up."

Daddy waited for just the right moment. And when he found it, he sat down, clasped his hands and lay them purposefully in his lap.

"Let me tell you a little story." He allowed just the right amount of time to pass. I was listening.

"One day Granddaddy set off up the mountain to cut some timber. 'Long 'bout the middle of the day one of the boys come runnin' back down the mountain hollerin' for Granny, 'Hurry! Come quick!'

Daddy stopped his story to remind me that people would come from all over for Granny's help. "She could cure fevers and set bones. Granny knew ever' plant and tree there was and what it was good for. Folks would pay her with a chicken or a bag of meal, whatever they had; Granny was a healer. If times were hard, she wouldn't take any trade, 'specially if it was their 'childern.'"

He continued his story in his distinct Kentucky brogue.

"Well, Granny looked through what she had and picked out a bag of sugar and a bucket of kerosene and set out for the timber. She walked a *waaay* on up that mountain 'til she found Granddaddy, layin' still as stone. Now, he was a sight. Tree had jumped the stump and caught him on the top of his head. Looked like he was already gone. Granny sat down on the ground next to him and began to work those healin' hands. She made a paste and put him back together with nothin' but sugar and kerosene."

The Gift

Daddy imitated how Granny worked the paste and kneaded Granddaddy's skin back to his body.

"Granddaddy never had a scar."

Lost in time, moved by her courage, something began to rise up in me from deep in my spirit.

Then Daddy said, "Honey, you're made out of good stuff." With that, he left me to my thoughts.

No better medicine could I have found.

What the doctors could not do, my family could. I never knew my Granny, but she spoke to me that day and I received a priceless gift. I knew that I could face my future and meet every challenge.

Granny **was** a healer; and one more time that bag of sugar and bucket of kerosene put a body back together. •

Lisa Miracle Ballard lives in Huntersville, North Carolina. An active volunteer and advocate in her community, her heritage inspires her writing which has been shared in community publications, newspapers, schools and churches. She is currently working on a collection of essays, poetry and short stories reflecting her Appalachian roots.

Death of a Mistress
by Susan Wilson

I hear the saw in the basement whine to a stop. His footsteps sound heavy for a man so small as he trudges up the stairs. Time for a break. I wait for the sound of his ring as it clinks against the blue-green bowl where he keeps his pocket change, his car keys, his lighter, and his pack of cigarettes. The sound never comes. Conditioned like Pavlov's dog, I am confused. And then I remember that he no longer uses the bowl. His key fob is in the drawer under the window. He no longer has pocket change. He no longer smokes. For years he would dip his hand in the bowl then slam the door as he left the kitchen and settled on the cushioned chaise lounge on the porch to pollute the air, stain his lungs, and stress his heart. Wind, cold, heat, rain, snow, or ice—none of those could prevent his rendezvous. Nicotine is a most demanding mistress.

I cajoled, pleaded, threatened, and shamed trying to get him to stop. I enlisted the help of our children. I printed off articles, quoted statistics, researched medication options. I insisted on restrictions: not in the house, not around the children, not in the car, not with me. I thought I could change him. But no barrier was unworkable; no constraint too severe. He told me he would quit eventually; he was thinking about it just not right now; then just stop, leave me alone. His mistress asked little; just a bit of his time. And a bit of his money. But a cardiac arrest, a week on a ventilator, three weeks lying in a hospital bed and fidgeting in a rehab unit, and suddenly his once tempting mistress looked like a hag.

For months he sat around, waiting for death to circle back and claim him. Certain he had cheated an opponent that would seek its revenge. Double or nothing. When death seemed to take a pass, I encouraged him to find something to do. Anything really. Work, play, hobby; I did not care. Just. Do. Something.

For now, he is working on finishing a room in the basement. I am working on my sanity. We do not need the space of course. The children are mostly grown. We have no need for playrooms or movie rooms or man caves. Resale value he says. Yes, and we need plenty of that. His income has been reduced to an early retirement age social security check and a distressingly small monthly pension. I missed weeks of work and months of opportunities tending to his health, tending to our finances, tending to appearances for the sake of our children. Rounding up lighters and discovering hidey-holes; abolishing the last traces of his old lover. My opportunities went elsewhere and like yesterday's news I sit in the recycle bin waiting for a chance to become something new. Hoping I am not destined to re-invent myself over and over again.

I read a story about a woman who was leaving her family for three months to spend the winter in a bungalow on an island—no neighbors, months of provisions, a generator if a winter snowstorm should knock out the power. She intended to meditate and write and understand herself. How enticing. How impossible. I cannot leave. I am the devoted wife, the one who stands by her man. For better, for worse, in sickness and in health. Or something close to it. Like most, his mistress was only around for the good times. And far more demanding than she appeared. When the storm came calling she packed up, blew a kiss, and hit the road before the first raindrop splattered the pavement.

I hear the basement door close and his footsteps thud down the stairs. Break time is over. I listen as he hammers the framing board into place while I type at the computer and do a cursory job search. His mistress was quite seductive, but in the end her calls go unanswered and she is left outside struggling with her umbrella, sodden and unattractive, slowly drowning, while I am curled up in the upholstered chair by the window watching the rain pelt the glass. •

Susan Wilson lives in Clemmons, North Carolina, and is a member of Winston-Salem Writers. She won the 2017 nonfiction award for WSW's anthology *Flying South* and was a finalist for the 2017 James Hurst Prize in fiction. She loves to write but unfortunately still has to keep her day job.

Can You Move It?

by Diane Pascoe

Whump!

Our youngest son's feet shot straight out from under him on the driveway. His screech could have raised the dead as he landed heavily on his arm. I knew it would be just a matter of time before those roller skates betrayed him, causing bodily injury.

He raised his arm limply in front of me as he winced. The arm looked normal to me. "Can you move it?" I questioned, in my best nurse voice.

He nodded.

"Then you must have just bruised it—let's get some ice on it." No need to dwell on every childhood ache and pain, right?

The next morning before summer camp, he complained that his arm was sore and maybe he shouldn't go to camp.

"Can you move it?" I asked again, just to double-check that my diagnostic skills were intact. He nodded. "Then you're fine. Off to camp now."

My office phone rang at 2:00 p.m. It was the camp counselor.

"Your son just tripped over a tree root and fell on his sore arm. He says it really hurts."

Jeepers...can that boy not stay on his feet for just one day? Is he determined to torment me? I packed up some of my office work and headed for camp.

His Royal Shortness was sitting on a log, rubbing the offending arm. "It feels much better now, Mom," he said as I reflected on all the work I'd just left behind at the office to tend to an arm that felt much better.

"Can you move it?" I inquired, asking the only medical question I knew to ask in such circumstances. He nodded. "Well, good. It's fine then."

"Do you think I should play in the soccer game tonight?" he wondered.

"Of course," I replied, sensing the start of a pity party. "You can't let your team down just because your arm is a bit sore. A little pain never hurt anybody, son."

I continued lecturing as only a mother can, hoping to teach him the importance of biting the bullet, sucking it up, and all the other metaphors meant to make men out of boys. That's my job, right?

The game warm-up began with our man-boy goalie in place, stopping each ball with his left arm, while the impaired right arm lay limply at his side. I admit it looked kind of peculiar.

Just as I was pondering this odd-looking scene, a soccer-ball missile hit his dangling right arm. That would be the same arm that he had assured Nurse Mom he could move and that I had assured him is fine.

My Love God, who had remained silent on my medical diagnostic technique to that point, said impatiently, "Do you think you could take him to the hospital to have it checked?"

Jeepers! Did my Love God grow up under a mushroom? Did he not receive the same medical education from his parents that I had—that if an arm can move, it can't possibly be broken? Are we raising a marshmallow or a man-to-be? Is no one listening? The boy can move it! He said so himself!

By then it was clear that I'd need to prove the soundness of my medical advice with a four-hour wait in the emergency room. We sat and sat. They finally x-rayed the limb, which had been laying like a wet noodle on his lap.

"What do you think is wrong, Mom?"

Testing one last time that it really was a moveable limb, I asked, "Can you move it?" He nodded. I felt like I had been

Can You Move It?

singing a refrain from a familiar song. "Then it's just a bad bruise, son."

The doctor appeared. "Mrs. Pascoe, your son has a broken arm and will need a cast on it for six weeks." His words pierced my heart.

"Whaaat?" I croaked. "But he can move it—isn't that the rule?"

Was my medical training flawed? Would child services be called and sentence me to baking brownies for the little man-boy whenever his stomach rumbled?

"Son, I am so sorry," I apologized. "I didn't know. Can you ever forgive me?"

"Sure, Mom—but can you please carry my backpack, shoes, coat, and books for me? I know it's heavy, but a little pain never hurt anybody."

Ouch. •

Diane and husband Eric, (aka "Honey" or "Love God"), retired to Leland, North Carolina in 2016 after many years in Raleigh. Along with winning several North Carolina writing contests, Diane's humor essays are published monthly in Wilmington-area publications.

Journey
by Elizabeth Chalfant

S ometimes you know how a journey will end and sometimes you don't.

Our well-planned journey from Kentucky to Oregon started in early fall, we headed west through the heart of the country to the beautiful Oregon coast by the middle of October. We visited our favorite scenes, knowing we would soon start the journey east, wondering when we would be back to these favorite places.

At 4 a.m., a nudge from my husband of 51 years brought me up quickly as he tells me, "It feels like there is a vice on my heart," not something anyone wants to hear, ever.

A new journey begins; there were no warning signs, and now no road map.

The hour's drive to Eugene from Florence is surreal. He always drives, always! Now he is the passenger, calmly telling me the pain is less, not radiating, and "actually not bad at all."

An emergency room visit, then to Oregon Heart and Vascular Institute in Springfield. This 73-year-old, who has never been hospitalized, now has the dreaded hospital gown, an IV, medications, and an appointment with cardiology in the morning.

The text message goes out to family and friends for the need of prayer and uplifting.

The next day Dr. Cook says, "I have good news; you're a healthy 73-year-old. And the bad news is you have three blocked arteries and we need to do triple-bypass surgery tomorrow with Dr. Koh."

This journey just took a real turn.

Calling our children to say your father will have major surgery in Oregon the next morning was hard, one of the hardest parts of this journey. They rearranged their lives, made reservations, and would arrive the evening of the surgery, not knowing what their journey to Oregon would bring them.

The day started early with surgery preparation, and at 6:45 the nurses in blue come to take him to the surgical floor. We talked and prayed during the night, assured each other it would be fine, and with a quick kiss, a squeeze of hands, he was off.

I am alone, in Oregon, with my husband going into serious surgery. I have a few tears but calmness throughout the day, knowing prayers over several states are supporting us.

Dr. Koh comes at 4 p.m., after a very long day, to say all is well and our journey will continue.

Our children arrive at 10 p.m.; they see their father at 10:30, groggy and blurry eyed, hooked up to so many machines, but smiling and glad to see them.

Tomorrow comes, and it is my 71st birthday. He looks great, sitting up and eating a full breakfast, laughing, telling me, "Happy Birthday." Best present ever.

We all know the parent-child role reversal will need to take place in a family at some point and today is that day. Our children's mission today is to find us a place to live four to six weeks as their father recovers. A daunting task made much easier by technology, which was our friend throughout this journey.

This day was saved by a single sheet of paper with rental information for places near the hospital. A photo texted, a cell call to the owner, the vehicle navigation taking them to the address. They were back in the hospital in a couple hours, smiles on their faces announcing, "We just rented you a house" and the journey could continue comfortably.

I admit I liked being taken care of.

Before flying back to their homes, the children were able to see their father take his first walk down the hall, see the house they had lived in decades ago, our pastor and his wife from their childhoods, and know we were in a good place for the duration of our stay.

The recovery time was pleasant and relaxing, visiting with

friends and enjoying the scenery along the McKenzie River.

One month from surgery Dr. Koh says, "You're doing great; enjoy your trip back to Kentucky."

Getting home was made much easier with family flying out to help drive the 2500 miles east, and the weather co-operated nicely.

Now he is a passenger in the back seat of his own vehicle and has to learn to watch the scenery and not the road. For the last 600 miles from Missouri to Kentucky it is my turn again; I must have passed the test as he took a nap on the way.

Our 2-month Western journey ended with a wonderful "welcome home" from family.

We acknowledge we were blessed with being in the right place, at the right time, with the right doctors and this journey was not something we could have planned. It was out of our hands.

Much blessed, our journey together continues. •

Elizabeth Chalfant lives in Winchester, Kentucky. She owns a business and volunteers in the community, including as treasurer of the Fort Boonesborough Foundation. This writing effort is her first attempt; it was inspired by the event and with the knowledge that the ending could have been so very different. The message, of course, is to "live every day to its fullest."

What I Don't Want To Write About Today

by Maureen M.

I don't want to write about the realization that came to me last week that it is time for me to tell my family about the sexual assault that happened to me as a child.

I don't want to tell my sister about what happened in the bathroom at the zoo while she was waiting outside. I don't want to have to remind her that she was right all that time when we were little and she was afraid to go to a public bathroom by herself because "there might be a bad man in there who will hurt us." We all got a little frustrated with her for making such a huge and inconvenient fuss over nothing. I need to apologize to her for not believing her, for not remembering, for not supporting the truth of her instincts. When I remembered the incident a couple years ago, I felt strongly that I should keep it to myself. But my guidance says it is time to share it now.

I don't want to tell my mother about my being sexually violated when I was young. She spent so much energy policing my posture, what I wore, and who I talked to, eliminating any signs of sexuality or sensuality or vibrant life force energy from my appearance, for fear of my "asking for trouble." How can I tell her that those efforts were way too much, way too late. That she was reacting to an awareness, however deeply buried, of something that had already happened, not something on the horizon that she could prevent with enough vigilance. I don't want to have to tell her I was raped and then watch her absorb the shock and feel the instantaneous and overpowering stab of her grief.

I don't want to tell my father that his youngest brother pimped 4-year-old me out to a heroin dealer in exchange for drugs. My uncle has been in and out of jail and treatment centers in connection with his drug addiction. And my dad has been there for him, providing bail money, housing, medical treatment, a car and tough love as needed. When my marriage ended, my dad said he didn't want to come out here to visit for a while because he wasn't sure he could resist the urge he had to go after my ex-husband. He was just kidding, I think. But he was raging at the hurt his little girl felt, and the impotence he felt about not being able to fix it. This is so much worse, or maybe this is really what he was reacting to. And I worry about how he will take it.

I don't want to have to confront my uncle about this either. And I don't particularly want his family to know. When I was back at my parents' house for Christmas, I saw a card from him to my parents. It had a picture of two of his four kids, and a note from his wife to my dad thanking him for being such a blessing to their family. I don't want to mess that up.

I realize that these thoughts are coming from a place of fear. A lot of fear. I am also feeling guilt. I feel guilty about upsetting the status quo, guilty about making other people uncomfortable. And then I remember that I can tell another story. A story of truth and power and healing. One that recognizes and honors the true essence of everyone involved in this circumstance, and their ability to receive this information with grace, and in the spirit in which it is offered.

What I do want to write about today

And so, what I want to tell instead is the story of what happened to me when I was young, how I healed from that, and the strength I developed from the experience. And I want to offer this story to everyone as a healing opportunity—to know the truth, to bring up from the depths of secrecy and shame the story that needs to be seen, that needs to be acknowledged by each person involved—so that it can be mined for the awareness waiting to be claimed by them, and so they can heal what needs to be healed in their life. Then the story can be released. I can let it go, we can all let it go, and it will no longer have a hold over any of us—body, mind or soul.

This is a story of freedom. •

Writing is a powerful act of healing for Maureen M. She believes that the stories we tell make a difference in how we live our lives. Maureen is happily writing the current chapter of her story in

Charlotte, North Carolina, and is grateful for the support of Charlotte Center for Literary Arts in helping to refine her writing skills.

My Mensch
by Susan Proctor

Wedged into my little Mercury Tracer, every inch packed tight, my son and I began the five-hour drive through eastern North Carolina tobacco country. We were headed home to Charlotte at the end of his first semester at East Carolina University. We had just pulled out of the dorm parking lot when he hit me with it.

"I can't come back." His voice was tight, fighting for control, but his next words brought the tears. "I got an "F" in math."

What a tough morning for him, dreading every hour that brought him closer to the moment he would have to face me and say those words. Though no kid relishes such a parental confrontation, for Benjy the stakes were much higher than my disapproval, although I suspect that was what he dreaded most. Sending him to college was not the fun family event it is for some—weekend visits to schools, applications in the mail, the excitement of opening acceptance letters, shopping, and writing the tuition check. A survivor of domestic violence, I have been a single parent since Benjy was four years old. He knew the nights I spent struggling under mountains of forms, week-ends researching at the library, endless phone calls to agencies with the power to bring tuition a few dollars closer. Half a house in my name and $1,000 above the poverty level rendered him "no need" by the standards set for government loans. College was nothing short of a miracle, made possible only due to a loan from Jewish Family Services and a Vocational Rehab scholarship based on his diabetes. We had no Plan B. Flunking math did not mean a stern lecture. Flunking math meant the end to college. To his dreams and mine. In Judaism there are two reasons for which it is permissible to sell a Torah. One is to get married, the other is to finance education. I had no Torahs to sell.

In that dark, crashing moment I found no cause for celebration. No proud benchmark of his first semester. It was going to be a very long drive home. Spasms gripped my stomach as my fingers gripped the steering wheel. Denial wrapped its protective cloak about me even while my brain screamed, "Fix this, fix this."

"Okay, Benjy. Here's what we'll do. We'll stay another day. And tomorrow I'll speak to your math teacher. I'll meet with every one of your teachers if I have to. They must understand exactly what hangs in the balance for you. And they'll help you. One of them will help you. One-tenth of a point is all you need to keep your money for another semester. One tenth of a point! You'll do an extra-credit project or you'll retake the exam. We can fix this"—meaning, of course, I CAN FIX THIS. After all, that's what mothers do, isn't it?

No matter. My rescue attempt was thwarted midstream by a voice resonating with new but unquestionable authority. "No. It won't make any difference. But the real thing is this: even if it would, I don't want you to, Mom. These are my grades. I blew my chance, not you."

He wiped the tears from his eyes and continued in a somewhat softer voice to lay out a plan. "I figure I can take history at the community college. It's a required course and my grade will transfer. I've already checked it out. I'll take that one class and I'll work to pay for it. I know I can make an "A" then I can ask for another chance next semester. But whatever happens, Mom, I promise you I won't quit."

I drove on in silence, not trusting myself to speak. Allowing my own tears to fall. Not four months ago he would have had a list a mile long of all the reasons why he failed, of all the people whose fault it was—the teacher who just didn't like him, the advisor who couldn't advise, the roommate who played his music too loud—a list with everybody's name on it but his. But now—no excuses. No blame. Just responsibility and a plan.

My fingers loosened a little on the steering wheel. I reminded myself to breathe. The stomach spasms eased up. This was not the boy I had brought to college. No, this was a mensch. Mensch is a Yiddish word reserved for those special few people whom we hold in the highest esteem, those who earn our deepest respect. I met such a young man on a sunny, crisp December afternoon on the campus of East Carolina University and in that moment of recognition, all the frightful years of being a single parent, feelings of inadequacy, sleepless nights paid their dividends in full. I had raised a mensch. •

Susan Proctor lives in Charlotte, North Carolina, and belongs to Charlotte Writers Club. Her love affair with words began early on, when as a student, she perked up at the sight of an essay question! She says, "After all these years later, I still get lost in words!" Her work has appeared in Lilith Magazine and Jewish Values Online, Literary Anthology of Mothers, Inc.

A Soldier's Heart

by Cynthia Briggs

When my grandfather died, he took his memories of World War II with him. My grandmother died 10 years later and as we cleaned out the house where they had lived for 63 years, I found relics of the war buried in dark corners and locked closets. Photos of him as a dirty-faced young man in uniform with a shock of black hair, his face serious, gun in hand. A shadow of the man I knew: Tidy and neat, wool cardigans and pressed slacks, white hair, smiling. Never with a gun.

Over and over I woke up at 3 a.m. wondering about this man I thought I knew. The need to understand was relentless. I reached out to a group of well-connected friends: Did anyone know of a World War II veteran who might talk to me? Who might help me know my grandfather all over again? One friend replied, "Yes." I interviewed one veteran, then another, then 90 more. I recorded their stories and donated them to a local oral history museum. It has been four years of conversations, and I am still haunted.

A World War II B-17 bomber flies over my neighborhood, in

town for the annual air show. It growls like an animal. It is impossible to look anywhere but up. I imagine a sky full of these planes, wing to wing, heading toward a target in Germany. I imagine how my grandfather felt as they flew overhead in 1945. It would have thrilled him. The lone plane thrills me now, and I am surprised to find I'm crying.

My friend John served as a tail gunner on one of those planes in the Pacific. On bombing runs, he crawled through a narrow tunnel, two feet in diameter, into a glass case, suspended in air, and took aim at Japanese planes. He remembers the oceans of fire beneath as they bombed cities. He thought of the women they killed, the little boys and girls and babies who never knew why they had to die.

Everett served in the Army as a medic. After D-Day, as the troops moved through France, they stopped for the night in an orchard. American planes flew low overhead, and the men waved in greeting. A mistake was made. Bombs were dropped. Friendly fire. Everett dove into his foxhole. Nearby, another boy was hit. Everett ran to assist him but knew it was too late. The boy's lung visible, Everett watched him breathe in and out until it was still.

I want to go back in time, to hear those planes flying overhead, the bombs falling. I know it's not logical. Every veteran I've interviewed has carefully explained to me that war is hell. They weep with remorse and grief from memories seven decades old.

And yet the longing remains. My life is spent in front of a

computer. I work and write online. I stream exercise videos and TV shows, movies, and social media. I want to fight for something. To live for something other than safety and entertainment.

Fred has piles of photos from his time in the Army: The flat, white snow in Belgium during the Battle of the Bulge. The jagged outline of destroyed cities. General Patton, who posed for him on the street. Dead babies in Buchenwald, after his division liberated the concentration camp. His smile disappears when he talks about that day, the overpowering smell of death and rot and disease. It stays with a man.

"I won't tell you everything I've seen," he explains. "No veteran ever will. There are things we saw, things that happened, that no person should ever know about, not even us." He's protecting me. I wish he wouldn't. I want all of it, the full spectrum of light and dark.

I am naïve to wish such a thing. For me, it's pictures in an album, stories. For them, it's embodied, the taste of iron, dirt, and filthy teeth, the crust of blood and mud drying on skin. Friendships gone in an instant, torn flesh and insides turned out. I'm seven decades removed and safe from the torment of it all.

All these men and women, they are slowly leaving me. Not just us, but me. It's personal. It's losing my grandfather all over again. Waves of grief crash over me and the sound of them hitting the beach is my own voice saying, "Don't leave. Don't go." Listening to their stories gives me courage and reminds me of the resilience of humanity. They have been intimate with fear and come through scarred, but stronger. Life has not truly tested me, not yet. Perhaps someday it will. Will I pass the test? I can only hope yes. •

Cynthia Briggs is a professor of counseling, an oral historian, and a writer of fiction and creative non-fiction. She is the co-editor of *Snapdragon: A Journal of Art and Healing* (snapdragonjournal.com). Her memoir and essays have been published in numerous print and on-line journals. She lives in Winston-Salem, North Carolina.

Shelby

by Landis Wade

My wife says my legal career is divided into two parts: before and after Shelby. And even though I practiced law for 14 years "before" and I'm approaching 20 years "after," the part in the middle—my four months in a Shelby courtroom—seem like the longest.

Before 1997, I knew only two things about Shelby, North Carolina. It was a small town on U.S. Highway 74 between Charlotte and Asheville and home to Bridges Barbecue, which dished out some of the tastiest chopped pork in the state.

The Shelby trial, as it became known in my family, was a defining moment in my legal career. My law firm rented every room in a local bed and breakfast to house the legal team, which included, me, two other lawyers, a paralegal, my secretary, an extra typist, a messenger, and the client representative. The B&B became home for six nights a week. At the age of 40, I had been to court many times, but I had never been lead counsel in a jury trial where the other side was asking for tens of millions of dollars. It should have been no surprise when I lost

15 pounds during the trial, eating light and worrying about the outcome.

Before the trial started, my wife and I planned a trip to take our young children to Disney World. We scheduled it for late October, four months after the trial was to begin, with plenty of time to spare. No North Carolina civil jury trial had ever lasted that long.

I learned quickly that a high stakes jury trial is an invigorating experience, an adrenaline rush full of highs and lows, much like an academic boxing match with 12 referees keeping score. Because I had no idea how the jury rated each punch and counterpunch, I laced up my wingtips every morning and just kept punching. And when the fight went the distance, I was exhausted.

The case involved bucket trucks. I represented the manufacturer of the cylinders that raised and held the buckets high in the air. The maker of the bucket trucks said the cylinders were defective. Many cylinders failed. Buckets crashed to the ground. The reason for the failure was the reason for the lawsuit. There were many witnesses. A battle of experts. And closing arguments, where each juror wore a black shirt when my opponent argued and a red shirt when I argued. Our team went nuts with that development. Someone found the classic book called "The Red and the Black," causing us to debate why a Shelby jury of mostly high school graduates or less would read what the book jacket described as a satirical portrayal of French society after Waterloo, full of monarchial corruption and greed. We later learned the jurors were "jerking the lawyers' chains" for keeping them in court for so long.

The jury rendered the knock-out verdict three hours before I boarded the flight to Disney with my family. Make believe land was what I needed most. My client had no further use for me and I was tired of rationalizing how we kept the damages much lower than expected.

In jury trials, there are no honorable mentions. My opponent, the winner, died recently, and his obituary said that he won "the longest civil jury trial in North Carolina history." It was like he was taking one last jab at me from the grave.

After the trial, I took a month off from work and built a deck. I worked with my hands, not my head. And while I was at it, I got a call from the nurse on the jury, the most educated of the bunch. She was in tears and wanted to meet with me, so we talked over a barbecue plate at Bridges. "I shouldn't have voted for plaintiff," she said. "I will sign an affidavit." I thanked her and explained the law in layman's terms: "What's done is done."

My 20-year legal life after Shelby was guided by the fact that I lost the longest civil jury trial in North Carolina history. The experience made me see scrappy losers in a positive light, but I had a hard time applying my "man-in-the-arena" empathy to myself. I came to fear losing cases like a person in bloody, sea water fears sharks; and, while that fear led to courtroom success, the sting of the loss was hard to shake.

We need a magic pill that halts second-guessing by people who live through tough trials. I should have listened twenty years ago to what I told the nurse over pork, slaw, and hushpuppies.

"What's done is done." •

Landis Wade is a North Carolina trial lawyer, a Charlotte Writers' Club board member, and the author of *The Christmas Courtroom Adventure Series*, three legal mysteries where Santa Claus believers are put on trial. He won the 2016 North Carolina State Bar short-story contest for *The Deliberation* and received awards in 2017 and 2018 for his non-fiction pieces, *The Cape Fear Debacle* and *First Dance*.

Bracing for Life
by Margarette Dunn

T he 1940s were tough. The aftermath of World War II had created grief and struggle globally as well as in Johnston County, North Carolina. Farm life meant hard work, but Mama's canning and innovative cooking skills shielded us from food shortages.

At the age of five, Mark, one of my four brothers, contracted polio, which resulted in muscle paralysis in his legs and forearms. He soon became able to move about only by scooting around on his buttocks and by pushing with his elbows. He had to be carried piggy-back to and from the school bus, as well as from class to class. Another brother carried him about during grade school; but, when he reached high school, Daddy contracted a kind, strong neighbor, who had the same class schedule, to carry Mark about the two-story school building. In our rural county, there was no support of any kind for people with physical disabilities, not even an elevator.

With the advancement of treatments championed by President Franklin Roosevelt and the virtual magic worked by our country-doctor family physician, Mark was admitted to the

Orthopedic Children's Hospital in Gastonia, North Carolina. He continued his intermittent education with bedside tutoring between the many surgical procedures and his rigorous physical therapy.

His determined spirit and his ability to overcome his troubles were demonstrated during one of his hospital stays. As a punishment for boyish mischievousness, Mark's bedtime snack was withheld. Undaunted, he climbed out of bed, pulled himself up and onto a gurney, and then wheeled himself to the kitchen, where he enjoyed his snack before returning to his room. They caught him during morning rounds when they saw his dirty casts. No more nocturnal trips to the kitchen! Though it got Mark into trouble this time, his innovative thinking helped him to help himself the rest of his life.

Returning from one of his extended hospital stays, Mark thought he would be able to walk without crutches or braces. This was a big deal and several friends were there to watch him demonstrate his walking skills. Unfortunately, he fell flat on his face. He was disappointed, and he knew this was how it would be for the rest of his life. So, he refused to go to school.

Daddy recognized this rebellion as a crossroads in my brother's life and knew it had to be dealt with. He simply picked up my brother and put him in his seat on the bus. Such action would probably be considered abusive today, but at that time, it was the only solution at hand. Mark just had to be educated! And, he was. Mark went on to graduate from Wake Forest College, now Wake Forest University, with a degree in education. He coached a middle-school basketball team from the bench, using the more talented players to demonstrate plays and to help their teammates.

Mobility and self-reliance improved for Mark with the new soft, padded braces with hinges that allowed him to bend his legs when sitting. The slip-lock hinge he and Daddy designed would slide down thus making the brace rigid with the shake of his leg. The new braces fastened with Velcro®; so did his new shoes. He was then a liberated man! I had fastened his braces and tied his shoes for many years during my teens.

Mark lived at home for a few years after graduating from college as he taught at a school nearby. My education was enhanced by his presence. At the end of my junior year, I found myself needing only one course to finish high school. Mark arranged for me to attend summer school, loaned me his car, and by midsummer, I graduated from high school! But with no plans! No money for college!

Mark asked me, "What do you want to do? Would you like to be a teacher or a nurse?" These were about the only two professions available. We decided I would apply to a small hospital nearby for nursing since it was nearby and not so expensive. Mark paid my tuition and deposited me in front of the nurses' residence. All those years of rubbing his legs with liniment paid off. I was on my way!

Years later, as we were recalling our life experiences, I asked Mark what was the most important development in his life. Without hesitation, he said, "Velcro®." I was amazed, but I understood. With Velcro®, he could fasten his own shoes and braces. This capability provided him the independence I took for granted.

In our world of troubles, big and small, the love of family is important, but sometimes, the simplest solutions can make the biggest differences in our lives. •

Margarette Dunn lives in Fayetteville, North Carolina, where she is a member of the "Write On, Right Now" writers group. She grew up on a farm in the post WWII era and is now a retired health professional. Margarette's story revolves around the struggles and perseverance of her brave, physically-challenged brother and his inspirational influence on her life.

The Trip Home
We Will Always Remember
by Carol Gearhart

B elieve it or not, we've made this trip many times since. It's never seemed nearly as long.

It was June 1986. My father had died that March and my husband, Brent, and I had flown home to Chicago for the funeral. My sister, eight months pregnant with twins, was not allowed to fly from Denmark so remained an ocean away from our grieving family. When the twins arrived in April, Mom went over to help. Once she returned home, I needed to see her pictures, hear her stories, and just be home to share missing Dad. Getting there turned out to be the first memorable challenge.

We left North Carolina after work Friday, overnighting along the road in West Virginia. The plan was to get to Mom's by Saturday dinner. Saturday morning, we headed north, winding along the beautiful Ohio River, the route we loved. We stopped at an antique shop and found a cupboard we simply had to have. Would they hold it until our return trip? Yes!

Continuing north about noon, suddenly we heard a loud explosion, and everything went black! Was it in the trunk? Then another boom! And another! Panic! We could not find the door handles to escape! Soon we realized our seat backs had broken and we had fallen flat on the floor looking up at the ceiling, our hands grabbing nowhere near the handles.

When we righted ourselves, the rearview mirrors reflected the car that had rear-ended us, its passengers frantically tossing beer cans into the ditch. Soon, a state trooper arrived and handcuffed the driver. We were informed he was so drunk he repeatedly rear-ended us trying to leave the scene.

The EMTs, arrived, fitted us with whiplash collars, and loaded us into the ambulance. The Cincinnati ER doctor proclaimed us injury-free but with whiplash likely. No fear, a new drug will allow you to continue your drive because "it does not cause drowsiness," he said! Exiting the hospital, we called a cab, found the nearest pharmacy to fill the Flexeril® prescription, then on to the nearest car rental agency. Turned out this was the cab driver's first day on the job and he called his supervisor multiple times for directions. When we finally arrived at the destination we found it was a remote maintenance office that did not actually rent vehicles. But, they kindly agreed to rent us a car with minor damage. Grateful for anything, we immediately headed back south to our stranded car.

Everything about it was warped and dented. Luckily a nearby garage agreed to store it. Headed north again, I called Mom saying we would not make it for dinner but would arrive that night. Then the Flexeril® kicked in.

Flexeril® may not make you drowsy, but it truly relaxes all your muscles! Brent drove 20 minutes before saying he could no longer hold his hands up to steer. I drove 15 minutes, then propped my elbows on my knees to support my limp arms on the wheel. Let's just say it was a long drive with a lot of stops!

We got to Mom's quite late. We apologized that we were beat and hit the bed without unloading the car.

On Sunday I arose late; the house was silent. I wandered out front to find Brent and Mom in the street, Mom saying, "It was late; you were on medication. Are you sure you didn't park down the block?" Brent, pointing down at the pavement, declared, "We parked right here in front of the house!" The car had been stolen!

The officers sat around Mom's dining room table and repeated their questions. No, we did not remember the car's make, year, or color. But we had the keys! Deciphering the abbreviations on the tag they concluded it was the local chop shops' favorite. We were tasked with going to O'Hare Airport to report the stolen rental car.

After waiting in a long line, we told the young attendant we were reporting a stolen car. She smiled, turned toward the adjacent attendant and whispered, "Trade customers with me!" Thankfully she whipped out the correct forms.

The rest of our stay was uneventful except for watching the Cubs in Wrigley Field using only eyeball action, without turning our sore necks.

The Trip Home We Will Always Remember

Readying to return home was another challenge. The other driver was uninsured. Our insurance company insisted we fly home, as it was cheaper, but what about picking up that irresistible cupboard? After multiple conversations, they relented, providing a one-way rental that would accommodate the furniture.

Relieved to be home in North Carolina, we soon received a check covering the value of our damaged car and its contents. Rest assured, we flew to Chicago for our next visit. •

Carol Gearhart grew up hearing treasured family stories, from short two-liners to long histories, continually retold at family gatherings. Then she married into another such family full of rich stories. Following her mother's lead, Carol now writes them down for future generations to enjoy. She and her husband reside in Pfafftown, North Carolina, in the home of Pepper, the cat.

No Forwarding Address
by Bruce Spang

My brother sat in a chair in the corner of the living room, a walker stationed by him. He smiled weakly at me. His legs, thick and covered with bandages, were exposed. I thought as I took him in, *He's dying*. I kissed him on the forehead.

"Hi, Skip, good to see you," I said.
"I'm not so good," he declared.
"I know."

He asked for some water. I sat across from him. We tried to talk as if nothing were wrong. We spoke of the good times when we were boys, the golf games, the tag football. He need-ed to go to the bathroom, but he could barely stand up. He lugged his oxygen tank with a long tube attached to it. A thin plastic hose ran around his head with two tubes stuck in his nostrils. I held the hose. He tried to hurry. His legs looked like tree stumps.

"I can't make it," he said.
"What do you want me to do?" I asked.
"Get me new pants," he said. "And underwear, in there …" He

pointed to his bedroom.

I helped him out of his pants and underwear, gave him a wash cloth to clean up, and put the pant legs over his feet so he could pull them up.

"It's so embarrassing," he said. "I'm sorry."

The next morning, Skip was dressed and had his oxygen tubes over his shoulder like a scarf when I arrived. He ate some cereal. After he finished, he looked at his watch. His counts were not good, he had said. Another hospital appointment.

"Time to go."

As he walked to the garage door, I stopped ahead of him, holding onto his long plastic tube so he would not trip on it. He looked at me. He sensed I was thinking the same thing he was. His eyes wandered from one object to another: paintings, TV, kitchen table, cupboards, sink, and free-standing granite table— taking it all in. Nothing was said.

He looked up. "You know, don't you?"
"Yes."
"Last time," he said.
"Yes."
"Thought so," he concurred, not moving. I stepped toward him.

He held up his hand. "No," he said. "It's all right."

He offered a weak grin.

"I …" My voice blundered into silence.
He said, "I couldn't do this without you, you know that."

"I do."

"Let's go." He glanced around once more at all that was his, and he nodded. "Well, that's it."

He asked, "Doc, how much time do I have?"

The doctor was a little surprised to get that question so quickly. He flipped through the charts. If Skip didn't mind, he said, he'd like to confer with the other physicians who were also in the room. They left and returned a few minutes later. The lead doctor talked in generalities about factors—if they could get his count down, if they could improve kidney function, six months, maybe more.

"My brother needs to know how much time he has right now," I said. "Is it weeks, days, a month?"

The lead doctor tightened his lips, said they'd do everything they could and left. The assistant gave the news. "Skip, I think you need to consider now the question of quality verses quantity." My brother grabbed my hand and squeezed it.

"And time?"
"Two, maybe three weeks."

Skip held onto me. They said how sorry they were, how much he meant to them as a patient willing to try a new regimen. The assistant said the lead physician had left because he felt their efforts were a failure.

Skip was hospitalized later that day to stabilize his kidneys and to drain off the fluid. He told them that he loved them all.

In the hospital room, after he got into the requisite hospital gown, he told me how frightened he was.

"It's not the dying. It's what happens after," he said. "Where do I go?"

That was THE question, was it not, the one we each ask at some point.

I asked him how many times he had moved in his adult life.

He added them up on his fingers. "Fourteen."

"Well, think about it," I said, trying to assuage his fears. "You left one place, moved away, leaving your job, your friends, and started over. This is another move."

He smiled warmly, "But this time, there's no forwarding address."

Every life touches others. No matter our paths or destinations, creating and keeping memories along our journeys are the business, the joy, the purpose of our living.

Thank you, Skip. I love you. •

Copyright 2018, Bruce Spang

Bruce Spang is former Poet Laureate of Portland, Maine. His new novel *Those Close Beside Me* comes out spring 2018. His first novel is *The Deception of the Thrust* (2015). His seven books include *Boy at the Screen Door* (Moon Pie Press). He teaches at the Osher Lifelong Learning Institute, UNC, Asheville. He lives with his husband, Myles Rightmire, in Candler, North Carolina.

You Can Do This

by Cherie Cox

"**D**on't be afraid, Charlotte. You can do this. Do what you know is right," he told her.

These words strengthened Charlotte Arnold Young. Her only brother, Oscar, lay dying from malaria, acquired while teaching in coastal North Carolina. They had supported each other emotionally and economically. They had taught in one- and two-room schools across the state in the early Twentieth Century.

"It will be hard without you," she said.
.

"You take that exam," he said. "Become a principal."

His failing eyes searched for the matching blue in hers. He touched her hand. He would never complete his cherished university education.

He had understood her dream of becoming a professional educator. At his death in 1910, she was a single woman in a man's world. Few women sustained careers beyond marriage.

I almost missed the opportunity to know Charlotte. My grand-mother's inadvertent remark that we had a poet in our family, led me to her cottage door in Asheville, North Carolina in 1976. By that time, she had brought literacy to generations. She had published books of poetry.

She greeted me as "Dear Cousin" and opened her life to me.

North Carolina's educational system was in its infancy when Charlotte became a principal. Hired by a new high school in Denver, North Carolina, she passed an examination to be certi-fied in 1912. Acting as principal her second year, she succeeded in improving attendance.

She explained how a woman's achievement cut two ways early in her career. A commissioner's tactless remark had left her speechless.

"Miss Young, you should be proud of your accomplishment here. Because of your hard work, we can afford to hire a man," he had told her.

"It was a woman's place to accept that gracefully in my day," Charlotte said. "I did, but it burned me up." Her pale blue eyes blazed, and her small frame stiffened every time she spoke of these memories, even as an octogenarian.

At an Appalachian school in Almond, North Carolina, one of Charlotte's appreciative students became a friend. Henry Alfred

Davis graduated from high school and joined the United States Army in 1917. His letters to his "Dear Teacher" during World War I improved his ability to write and read. His own father, a skilled mountain craftsman, had been illiterate. Henry promised Charlotte that he would not be afraid and that he would come home safe.

By the time Henry returned, the school had hired a male principal to replace Charlotte. But she remained resilient and taught school into her eighties in five different states. Whenever asked her age on her employment applications, she simply wrote "atomic."

"I am not afraid of change," Charlotte told me, as she approached the last of her 107 years. She had outlived that young soldier, who had been my grandfather. Henry Alfred Davis had married Charlotte's young cousin and had become a respected teacher himself.

The same standards Charlotte held in teaching, she held in poetry. Six published books, with titles including *The Heart Has Reasons* and *Thunder in Winter*, affirmed her passion for the writing craft. For more than half a century, North Carolina's best poets received the Oscar Arnold Young Poetry Award. She had founded this memorial to her brother during her service as president of the state's Poetry Council in the 1950s. Despite her prominence in the art of verse, so far she has been the only poet in the family.

"I'm writing another book of poetry," she said, during one of my visits in the late Seventies. At the time, I had an offer to

You Can Do This

practice law in Charlotte, North Carolina. It would have meant leaving Asheville, where I had struggled in seeking employment, but where I could have stayed near Charlotte, the poet, and my grandmother.

She began typing on her nearly ancient Underwood typewriter. I heard every keystroke hit the paper. I sat, waiting for her wisdom.

She read her poem, "Clean Break," then handed it to me.
"You can't live on broken dreams," she read.
"Take the new road." •

Cherie Cox covered news for the Hickory Daily Record before she served as an assistant public defender in Charlotte, North Carolina. Her poetry placed first in the 2002 Charlotte Writers' Club's competition. Current published works include this essay, a short story, and several poems.

Complete: A Walk of Faith
by Arnetta Freeman

There she was, Dr. Abbey, standing over me with her team. A 5-person, uniformed, scrub-wearing, surgeon-support team waiting to get their hands on me. The goal: to stop the bleeding. Her team rattled off a list of questions like I was ordering takeout. What are you having today, a full or partial? Would you like a blood transfusion? Do you want to be resuscitated? Do you have a living will? "I don't know. Yes. Yes. No," I answered. After taking my order, one of them said, "Alright dear, sign here," and they exited.

I would have done anything to get out of the white, sterile box they had wheeled me into, and to trade places with my ex-husband who was sitting uncomfortably for the past hour in the chair next to my bed. He struggled to stay awake and tossed his head from side to side in each palm creating his own head rest. The rapid beeps from my heart-monitoring machine forced him to awake and to be present in my crisis. "Looks like you've come unplugged," the nurse announced as she entered the room. I had indeed.

My restlessness from being awakened at 5:30 a.m. combined

with my indecision about being cut horizontally at my bikini line and fears of losing both my agility and womanhood caused me to unravel. This was not supposed to be happening to me, I reasoned lying there. I was the healthiest 48-year-old African American I'd known. I was free of daily meds, and of my family's history of diabetes and high blood pressure, and in near perfect shape. Why hadn't I escaped this? Endometriosis. Translation: surgery. The word beeped in my mind as intermittently as the equipment that was monitoring my vitals. "It looks like your blood pressure is up a bit," the nurse announced. An hour later, I still had not come to terms with the idea of a "Hys-te-rec-to-my."

The uncontrollable bleeding required a rapid response, leaving me little time to think. The nurse came back announcing they were ready for me. "So how are you doing dear?" The teardrops rolling down each cheek answered for me, *Not well*.

"Don't worry, hon. It'll be ok," she assured me. "Lots of women have them. It's a routine surgery. No big deal. They'll have you in and out in a jiffy," she continued and began exiting. Despite her assurances, "the big deal" was my deal. I was ready for the bleeding to stop, but not to lose the one thing I believed made me a woman. "Can I speak to the doctor again?" I said nervously. "Sure, you can, dear," she answered. "I'll get her for you."

When the surgical team re-entered, my husband and I looked at each other, neither smiling—the same way we looked at each other when I announced, after trying to reconcile, that I couldn't do it anymore and was going through with our divorce.

Similar fears played into my consciousness. How was I going to come out once this was over?

Dr. Abbey walked in like a 3-star general, wearing her badge and an equally stiff smile. You wanted to see me," she announced. "What happens if I don't have the surgery?" I asked in tears. Her response was as cold as the rail I gripped onto. "Well, you could go home and die," she declared without hesitation. So, I could die if I don't have the surgery and die if I do, I reasoned to myself, daring not to speak back. Despite her coldness and my worst fears, I closed my eyes and did not open them again until I heard my ex standing over me say, "I think she's waking up now. Thank you so much Dr. Abbey."

I never thanked Dr. Abbey, but I did thank my ex-husband for standing with me during the three months that followed on bed rest during my recovery to regain muscle and to walk again. My marriage did not survive, but we renewed our friendship. In bed, I had time to think about how life can throw you a curveball like divorce and surgery. And despite not having all the answers about how I would come out on the other side, some things you just have to do by faith.

One year later, I celebrated my agility by walking in a 5k race for breast cancer. I walked alongside women, breastless. Others hairless. Me, with one less ovary. Each of us still a woman. Raising awareness was only one of my goals. Raising my own consciousness about what it means to be a woman, my other. With each and every step I took, I was confident that I would cross the finish line complete, with one less ovary (thanks, Dr. Abbey) and with a lot more faith. •

Complete: A Walk of Faith

Arnetta Freeman lives in Winston-Salem, North Carolina, and is a member of Winston-Salem Writer's Group. She has published a children's book, *Play Brelyn Play, Dance Angels Dance*; she is currently working on another. She also has a poetry book and journal currently in publication; *No More S.I.S.* inspires young women to overcome adversity when facing domestic violence.

Me Alone
by Valerie Paterson

Women today bravely, and finally, have pioneered the #Me Too movement. I lived in the Me Alone days, falling victim to such vulnerability several times in just a few days and then again a decade later.

After ending my responsibilities as an *au pair* in Brittany, France, I accepted an overnight ride to Paris with a friend of a friend, Karantin, who was a rather average-sized man in his late twenties. Since I could not view any French Chateaus or picturesque vineyards in the dark, I fell asleep.

I was suddenly awoken to find my shorts and underpants being pulled down, already midway down my thighs. Karantin had come around to the passenger side of the car, his pants down, and was quickly on top of me in the biblical sense. This was rape. Premeditated rape. Rape in the middle of nowhere—a country road in the middle of farmland, in the dark, in the middle of the night with no one around. It all happened so quickly.

What should I do? Where could I go? My only possessions in the country of France were my heavy, cumbersome suitcase and awkward train case. I could barely pick them up, and I didn't think I could carry them for who-knows-how-many miles in who-knows-what direction. We were in the middle of farmland in the middle of the night. Afraid, and with no other choice, I stayed in the car to get back to Paris.

Once in Paris, I went to see Ben, my yoga teacher and friend. I climbed the daunting flights of stairs to his 6th floor apartment. I knocked. He was there. *Thank goodness.* He welcomed me in and I told him all about what had happened—the ride back to Paris and the rape.

Ben listened as I told him the story. Then he grabbed me, tried to kiss me and I was *horrified.* I told him to let go, but he wouldn't. *Is he thinking he can rape me too? Let me go! Stop! Arretez!* I struggled and got away. I ran ... and ran, spiraling down six flights of narrow stairs. Fear soared through my body. *Was he coming after me?* I just kept running to get away.

Now what? With no one to stay with in Paris, I took a train to Switzerland. As I walked along the river in Lucerne, a man who spoke German and Italian approached me. Speaking only English and meager French, I discouraged any further interaction with him. I made my way back to my small hotel, unlocked the outside door and slipped in; but, I could not get the door shut before this man pushed his way in.

This was *déjà vu.* Like Ben, this jerk was now grabbing me, in the vestibule of this small hotel. While my being petite may have made me attractive to him, it was my disadvantage in hand-to-hand combat. *Kick him in the balls. Kick him!* That was easier said than done. *Maybe my knee could do the job.* I kept kicking and fighting him off until I managed to get through the second door into the hotel, leaving his aggression rebuffed, his lust unmet, and him perhaps a good bit damaged.

Why did these men attack me? I was a cute, small female, probably a factor for Karantin as I slept in his car. And Ben? I thought he was a friend. Friends don't grab like that. This was not a caring hug from a friend who understood my pain. Did he think I was now fair game since Karantin had his way with me? Is that how French men think? As for the jerk in Lucerne, did I have a sign on my back that said *me voilez?* Rape me? No! I did nothing to encourage any of these men. I did nothing to deserve this. … And, I did nothing to stop them from ever accosting other women either.

Nine years later, I was raped again, at knifepoint in my Boston apartment by a serial rapist. The police asked if I would testify in court. I gave them an unequivocal "yes." This time I would help protect other women.

Two other victims and I met with the district attorney on several occasions to bring the rapist to justice. I relied on my inner strength to overcome my post-traumatic stress during those two years. The rapist received a life sentence. I closed the door on that episode and went on with my life. But, for years the trauma lay dormant, hiding within. I didn't—I couldn't—speak about it … until a chance meeting with one of the other victims helped give me voice. I could talk to her. She understood.

Now, I can speak about it. I should. I will. •

Valerie Paterson lives in Greensboro, North Carolina, where she is in a Memoir Critique Group, part of Writers Group of the Triad. She has written snippets of her life in her head, many of which are now becoming more real on paper. She loves to design and make quilts and to dance the Argentine Tango.

Finding Rebecca Boone

by Kiesa Kay

Rebecca Boone's resilience inspired me to set everything else aside and follow her trail through time. Loneliness lifted when this hard-working frontier woman stepped from the shadows of her larger- than-life husband into my mountain cabin. Her struggles and strength formed the foundation of my new play, *Love Makes a Home: The Life of Rebecca Boone*.

Rebecca Bryan Boone, a frontier woman, midwife, and the helpmate of America's pioneer hero, Daniel Boone, endured one hardship after the other. During her 74 years lived mostly back in the 1700s, Rebecca moved more than 20 times. She gave birth to ten children and raised at least four children born of other mothers. Two of her sons died violent deaths, and one in infancy. One daughter was kidnapped—and rescued. Her husband, Daniel, traveled far to hunt and explore, often for years at a time, leaving her to fend for herself with all those children on the fringes of civilization. Her mother had died early in her life, and her grandparents raised her, moving from Virginia to the Yadkin River Valley when she was only ten years old. She met Daniel Boone at a frolic when she was 16.

He lost every penny he made and every acre of land he owned, but Rebecca stayed with him and loved him through every anguish.

I first found Rebecca Boone at a Kiwanis meeting in Tryon, North Carolina, in 2013, where I was giving a speech about preventing child abuse. The executive director of the Tryon Fine Arts Center and I got to talking about what dreams we still had in our lives. She had wanted to be an actress, she shared, and had dreamed all her adult life of being Rebecca Boone on stage.

Well, I write plays and often help dreams come true. So began a journey that has yet to end. I read voraciously, gobbling up books about Daniel, poetry about Rebecca, children's books, Daniel Boone's letters, and hundreds of online accounts of all kinds. I learned that a friend of a sister had been in a TV-series about the Boones. I even found a Rebecca Boone Cookbook, with recipes purportedly handed down from Rebecca herself.

I've been a wanderer, and Rebecca's life resonates with me. When I first found her life story, I lived in a lake cabin on Melrose Mountain in North Carolina. That winter grew bitter cold, and I was snowed in alone for eight days, with only my dog, Rosa, for companionship. The wind at night howled like a shrieking banshee beating against the windows. Unbeknownst to all until after the ice melted, a neighbor lady had tripped, bumped her head, and died of exposure less than a mile from me. Even with summer arriving a sadness crept deeper into my heart with more deaths, as close family passed away.

A family friend drove me to a distant Kansas funeral. He suggested visiting Nathan Boone's house in Defiance, Missouri, and the Daniel Boone National Forest. He took me to the Yadkin River Valley to play my fiddle, and I made later treks to Kentucky and Tennessee.

Rebecca had known loss so intimately, and in this year of constant sorrow, she became my true companion. I felt her by my side every time I sat down to write. Soon enough, Rebecca and I had written *Love Makes a Home*. With the addition of historically authentic fiddle tunes by my friend, Bruce Greene, the play became complete.

A play is a work of art, creating connections and indelible images. For the audience's sake, I had to omit much material, condensing a vibrant life story into a contiguous and meaningful whole, conveying the essence of this woman – her strength, her compassion, her resilience. I crafted the play as a monologue, strongly rooted in historical fact. I had been painstaking in my research. Details surrounding one of her pregnancies came into contention among scholars, and I followed my intuition in choosing how to tell the tale. Rebecca herself neither read nor wrote, so her words have not been left as a guide.

Three actors – Barb McEwen, Patti Louise Smith, and Marianne Carruth – have portrayed Rebecca Bryan Boone in *Love Makes a Home*, in diverse venues. Each actor brings a new depth and intensity to the play. Barb plays her as a strong, devout woman. Patti shows Rebecca's sensual side. Marianne portrays her as a loving mother. The three actors speak the same words, but in different voices, and each one gives Rebecca new life.

Rebecca suffered many losses, but she kept her deep love for her family and her abiding faith in God. Two hundred years after her passing, she became my true friend—a remarkable, enduring, and endearing woman—Rebecca Bryan Boone. •

Kiesa Kay, poet and playwright, lives in a cabin in the Appalachian Mountains. Her play, *Love Makes a Home: The Life of Rebecca Boone* has been presented at the Orchard at Altapass and several other venues in North Carolina and Kentucky. Kiesa leads writing workshops and plays old time fiddle. She can be reached at kiesakay@gmail.com.

Bobby Got His Butt Kicked

by Randell Jones

ey, fatty."

"Leave me alone."

"Who's gonna make me?"

"I will, . . . damnit."

"Like hell, pudge boy."

The cry went up from the athletics field, "Fight!"

I'd not seen too many fights up close. I'd tried to keep a safe
distance from such violent encounters. Still, tales of flowing
blood, loose teeth, and torn clothing abounded. That's how
those neighborhood scrapes and after-school brawls got to be
such honored touchstones of our difficult passage from boyhood into manhood in the mid-1960s.

Bobby had finally had enough. He'd decided it was sink or
swim. Show the bullies he could take what they could dish out
or be prepared for the rest of his life to be under the thumb of
people just a little bit bigger and quicker, or just plain meaner

than he was. Bobby was standing his ground. That was a big mistake.

Larry was as bad as they came in our neighborhood. He was the loveless product of a broken home, if that's what you call it when the parents still live together but date other people and bring home strangers for a beer in the bedroom while the other one is away. So, Larry had pretty much reared himself; and, he was well studied at the school of hard knocks. He hadn't learned much else, but he'd mastered the art of fist fighting.

Bobby had just been standing around on the athletics field behind the junior high school cafeteria after lunch, the boys outside, the girls inside. Bobby didn't say much most of the time and he didn't have many friends either. He was a little heavy, not too tall, and not so fit. We all knew that made a guy an easy target, so we all believed in safety in numbers. To Bobby that meant a bunch of us would likely stick up for him against a bully. But, to the rest of us, "safety in numbers" was more akin to being not so readily distinguishable to a lion stalking a herd of antelope on the Serengeti Plain. Blending into the crowd reduced our chances of being singled out by a predator. Same rule of thumb, different application. Apparently, ours was working; Larry was picking on Bobby.

Bobby leaned forward and stuck out his chest with his head up and his chin thrust forward. He was on the tips of his toes trying to look as tall and as defiant as his 5-foot-2-inch, 140-pound frame would let him. That's when Larry shoved him, and Bobby put up his fists. Bobby's fists weren't big, and they weren't fast. They were soft and not at all calloused as Larry's were from frequently striking the faces of other people.

Bobby squared up and shuffled into a fighting stance, looking every bit afraid. He thrust his left arm forward, but Larry was bobbing and weaving. Larry crouched down as Bobby's fist went outward where Larry wasn't. Bobby had left himself open. Larry sprang up, threw two quick left jabs with a brick-hard fist. Both punches landed in the same spot—just above Bobby's right eye squarely on his forehead. Bobby never saw them coming.

In just three seconds, Bobby had a swollen, dark blue knot on this forehead as big as half a baseball. Bobby dropped his guard, covered his face, and stumbled backward to escape the ferocious predator. The fight was over. Fact was, it never had begun.

Bobby went home that day and probably tried to explain what had happened. He might have claimed he was hit by a bat during a softball game or maybe that he tripped and fell while changing classes. Who knows? He might have told his parents the truth. The problem was, just like the rest of us guys, he was trying to be a man in a boy's world. He was trying to prove something to everybody else and mostly to himself. He was trying to define who he was for the rest of his life, so he'd never again have to back down, turn tail, and run.

Bobby died that summer. He drowned while swimming in a lake. Bobby never made it to the 10th grade. He never had a date or kissed a girl or got to drive a car. He never got to drink a beer, cast a vote, or fight in Vietnam. He missed all the chances the rest of us had to prove that we were men. He missed them all, except the one he took when he picked his own time.

Bobby was a kid, but a brave kid even if just that once. He might have gotten his butt kicked, but for me that was the day Bobby became a man. •

Randell Jones lives in Winston-Salem, North Carolina. He is the author of several award-winning history books, including *In the Footsteps of Daniel Boone*, and two videos. Since 2007, he has served as an invited member of the Road Scholars Speakers Bureau of the North Carolina Humanities Council. He writes, speaks, and publishes as Daniel Boone Footsteps at www.DanielBooneFootsteps.com or www.RandellJones.com.

From Dreams to Realities
by William H. McCann, Jr.

February 2, 1958 changed my life. Before, I had been a normal, happy child—meeting and exceeding early childhood milestones. But on that Sunday, I had the first of many epileptic seizures that destroyed "normal " and changed everything for both my parents and me.

Later diagnosed as myoclonic seizures (today the diagnosis would be Doose Syndrome), what I actually experienced were grand mal and petit mal seizures, accompanied by jerks and falls which collectively were debilitating and nearly constant. For almost a year I wore a football helmet for protection. Then, miraculously, the seizures stopped.

Afterwards, I was brain-damaged and physically uncoordinated—walking like Frankenstein and slurring my speech because I drooled. Treatment included phenobarbital and other barbiturates—up to 26 pills a day—which created their own consequences.

Flash forward four years: I was six years old and had been kicked out of every kindergarten in Lexington, Kentucky. I still had an undetermined amount of brain damage, an inability to sit still, poor speech skills, and even worse coordination. My parents sought out—along with my tutor, Peggy Leiterman— educational options. There were no "special education" classes anywhere in Kentucky. So, Ms. Leiterman looked beyond Kentucky and found the Cove Schools of Racine, Wisconsin and Evanston, Illinois.

The residential Cove Schools in Racine was where my parents sent me. Beginning March 1, 1962, I lived not at home with my family—then two siblings and my parents—but in a large, drafty, gothic-style church building that resembled Ludwig Bemelmans' Parisian house for Madeline. The buildings looked much alike and though her 11 schoolmates were fictional, my 23 were quite real. For a little more than four years—from March 1, 1962 to June 15, 1966—I lived in Racine, at the Cove Schools, except for summers and a few weeks at Christmas.

Looking back, its teachers and students saved my life. It is hard to convey what the experience was like. But while there I regularly wrote letters home and those, plus poems written later, look back at the events of that time painting pictures of what it was like to be away at school so young:

"Letter: April 11, 1962"
Dear Mommie and Daddy,
We got up early yesterday morning.
We boarded a big orange school bus and went to Chicago.

We went to the Museum and I saw a lot of machines.
I saw how baby chicks come out of the egg.

We saw ducks, pigs and a farm.

We went into a coal mine to see how they get coal.
They showed us how it works for a fire.
We saw a lake, we saw clouds, and heard it thunder,
Saw it lightning and rain.

All of us ate in the cafeteria. Mr. Bartlett asked me to help
him. I went and got napkins for the children like a big boy.
I had a good time.

I fell asleep on the bus on the way back to school.

Love and kisses, Bill

Everything that has happened since was made possible by the
Cove's rigid schedule that calmed me, and eventually eliminated
any hyperactivity. The small classes of six to a room—with
each student facing a wall—and techniques such as flannel
boards and constant repetition helped ensure academic success.
But I think it was the fact that we students did not know how
difficult our paths ahead were; we believed in ourselves, in our
natural inevitability to attend college and have normal lives.
Many mornings we discussed such subjects among ourselves,
not knowing that our teachers and parents thought such things
impossible (certainly not inevitable).

"Dreamers"

Doug could not hear—
        Twin hearing aids turned up full
        Said as much.

From Dreams to Realities

I struggled with walking, balance, playing ball
    And social skills
    Not to mention an IQ of 62.
Joe, Tommy, Steve and I talked of
    College, career and family.
Our teachers and parents
    Would have laughed.

Before leaving the Cove, my parents were told my "success"
might be limited; "He might never graduate from high school."
Back in Lexington I was enrolled in a "regular" classroom two
years behind my peers. Yes, I struggled socially and academically.

Yet I succeeded.

I was in the top-third of my high school class. I earned a BA
in history, and graduate degrees in education and theatre, then
had careers in teaching, theatre and writing. I married and had
a son who is now succeeding in his own career. In my mind,
my Cove friends and our early morning conversations explain
my success in high school, college, and beyond. We were certain of our destinies; of course, they became our realities. •

Bill McCann, Jr. is an editor, publisher, teacher, playwright, and poet. He is a member of the Dramatists Guild; with Jeanine Grant Lister, he is co-leader of the Grant County Writers Group, Williamstown, Kentucky. He is the editor of *Kentucky Theatre Yearbook, 2018* and of *I Come From: A Voices Inside Anthology*. He lives in northwest Harrison County, near Corinth, Kentucky.

The Making of a Warrior Woman
by C. Kay Jones

I don't remember being told fairy tales when I was little. Even if I had heard them, I no longer had room for any. I was too consumed with starry fantasies of romance, love, and sweet embrace. I dreamed of one who would love me enough to lift me out of the pit of sexual abuse and helplessness I'd struggled for years to rise above.

At age 19, I married a man who already abused me. Bruises, black eyes, and sexual violence were the harsh realities of my home life. The only beauty from that union was our two sons and one daughter. The injuries they suffered at his hands fueled my resolve to find safe refuge for us all. When the opportunity was right, I grabbed it. The 60 days required to complete the divorce was fraught with his terror tactics and his raping me twice. We hid ourselves from him with friends, but one week after the divorce proceedings, he found us. He mercilessly tried to beat me to death in front of our small children.

Although I was terrorized, I faced my ex-husband's threats and vowed with hopeful expectation, "No more starry dreams for me, only truth." Truth brought no comfort, however, and I again went searching for romance, love, and sweet embrace. Two years later I married Jeff, who was a much-loved member of his church. I felt safe and protected. Abuse, however, has many faces. And abuse carried out under a cloak of feigned religious convictions generates woundedness only God can make whole.

In 1983—a decade into my marriage to Jeff—my adopted daughter, Marion, 14, told me Jeff had sexually molested her many times since she'd come to live with us five years earlier. If I thought it could get no worse, her sweet lips proved me wrong with nine more biting words: "He also molested Sarah when you first got married." (Sarah, my biological daughter, was 8 years old when we wed and was then 17.) I had never heard of child molestation or pedophiles. Had I been informed, I just might have recognized the textbook behavior that brings so much misery into the lives of those affected by it.

Jeff was indicted on these and two more revealed counts of sexual child abuse. He was sentenced to prison for two consecutive terms of one to five years. He held me emotionally captive during his incarceration with countless pleas for Christian forgiveness. After the fact, I know he was convincing because he used my past insecurities and my faith to create the illusion that he had changed. When Jeff was out on a work release program, I visited him, determined to decide whether to stay married or to divorce him. Our visit at the local mall confirmed the answer I suppose I'd known all along. During our conversation, Jeff grew quiet and stopped talking. I turned and saw the real face of a pedophile. His eyes were transfixed on two young girls standing directly in front of us. He was oblivious to me or anybody else in the mall. My soul cried out, "I cannot live with this the rest of my life! No more! At any cost, no more!"

Fast forward 35 years—chock-full of intense counseling and fervent prayer—I am married to Jerry, who respects my gentle ways and from day one has encouraged me to stand up for myself. The road leading to the present has been long, paved with firm commitments, strident perseverance, intercessory prayers, and many tears. Just learning that I was a full-blown pleaser opened a whole world of self-discovery and new understanding. My regret for the years lost to my indecision strongly validates that my passive acceptance of my painful circumstances was never easier than whatever steps I could have taken to resolve and eliminate the dis-ease. It now feels empowering to say "no" or to disagree with someone, healthily and without fear. It feels wonderful to be, well . . . free!

I have shared this story with the hope that my transparency might resonate with someone's current or future situation and save a child from the devastating scourge of molestation and sexual abuse. I always knew faith played a big part in my recovery. Through writing about my experiences, I recognized countless good things God was accomplishing in the very midst of my darkest days. When a dear friend said to me, "Kay, you're the only person I know that could find something beautiful at the dump," I knew that was the appropriate title for the story of my transformation: how God did His part to make a warrior woman out of an abused and vulnerable—but somehow resiliently brave—young girl. •

The Making of a Warrior Woman

C. Kay Jones is a Christian author, singer/songwriter from Greensboro, North Carolina. She earned top Gold Status in Outstanding Essay for the 2016 Second Spring Literary Anthology. Her writing appears in *50 Great Writers You Should Be Reading*, 2013-2014 Edition. Her Memoir, *Something Beautiful at the Dump*, epitomizes God's promised recompense for maintaining integrity with Christ during extreme losses.

The Day I Was Fired

by Diane Pascoe

I'm going to be flat-out honest with you. I was fired once from a position I had always wanted. It was the supreme failure of my life to that point. I had no one else to blame, though goodness knows I tried. With this firing, I entered the Hall of Shame, where you get to ponder your failures for the rest of your life.

Being fired hasn't been my only failure, of course. Being divorced also suggests loser behavior, but I jointly own that one with my ex, Mr. Wrong, and as you'd probably guess, I believe he owns the bigger share of the blame. Well, that's my story, and I'm sticking to it.

When I first got the f-word from the boss, I was stunned. I was fired in front of my peers. I sobbed. It was my dream job because it possessed fame, glory, and prestige. I loved the position, though in retrospect, I was wholly unprepared for the responsibility, the technical requirements, and the spotlight it put me in.

I remember f-day like it was yesterday. I can vividly recall that my brown hair was cut in a bob, with crooked bangs sloping from left to right. I could imagine what the neighbors said: Lordy, did that girl get her hair cut by the hairdresser or the dog groomer? Even I, a four-year-old, knew I looked weird.

Yup—I was four years old when I was fired.

The nightmare happened when I was in the kindergarten rhythm band. I was usually relegated to banging two sticks together or clanging the triangle. I didn't like playing the sticks. I wanted to be the lone glorious drum pounder or the tambourine shaker, not a crummy twig tapper.

Then one day my teacher, Miss Coyle, asked me if I'd like to be the band conductor. You know, like Ricky Ricardo or Mitch Miller. My flat chest puffed up; my shoulders went back. I was handed the baton, led up to the platform, and turned around to face my kindergarten band—a sea of hopeful faces staring at me.

Now this is the point at which it all started to go wrong. I had no idea what I was supposed to do with that flipping baton. I had seen Ricky and Mitch on TV, but with severe four-year-old performance anxiety, I couldn't recall if they twirled it, tossed it, or drew circles with it. I just stood there, baton arm frozen at my side, and started to cry.

Miss Coyle grabbed the baton and started waving it wildly, while the twig-tapping girls began banging their wooden instruments of musical torture. The tune ended, and I slipped away to my seat on the floor, head down, silent.

The next day the teacher called me up to the platform and handed me the baton once again. But I still didn't know what to do with that darn baton. So, I cried—again.

Then came the final insult. The teacher called on Raymond, who hadn't even learned how to tie his shoes yet, to take over my job. I had no warning, no probation. She just passed him my baton and asked me to sit down with the rest of the faceless, nameless stick bangers. Then Raymond started waving the baton just like I'd seen the conductors do on TV.

Please, Miss Coyle, I get it now!

I desperately tried to catch the teacher's eye to show her the light had finally come on. But she had eyes only for Raymond, leaving me in the corner with my sticks. I was yesterday's news.

For more than fifty years, I've been swinging that baton in my dreams to see if I could get it right. I can't read a musical note or carry a tune, and my pitch has been off since the birth of my first child. Music was never going to be my career, so my baton failure was probably inconsequential in the scheme of things.

But here's the important stuff that I learned in Miss Coyle's class:

> • I learned that firing is just the umpire telling you that you lost the game when all along you were playing poorly and probably knew how it would end anyway.

The Day I Was Fired

- I learned that with a bit of help, people could learn to do their jobs much better.
- I learned that career success is possible when your career goals fit your strengths. In other words, don't try to swim upriver—that's for fish.
- I learned that pain dulls with time, and humor carries the day.
- I learned that failures are where life's lessons are learned, so celebrate failure as a character builder.

See—I really did get it, Miss Coyle. •

Diane and husband Eric, (aka "Honey" or "Love God"), retired to Leland, North Carolina in 2016 after many years in Raleigh. Along with winning several North Carolina writing contests, Diane's humor essays are published monthly in Wilmington-area publications.

Blue Skies in a Cyclone

by Valerie Macon

I t was an ordinary Friday afternoon drive home from work when my cell phone rang. The woman on the other end said she was calling from the Governor's Commissioners Office on behalf of the Governor to ask if I would serve as North Carolina Poet Laureate. Although I had been writing and sharing poetry as long as I can remember and had published two books of poetry, I was not intimately familiar with the position of poet laureate. I did an internet search on the topic and realized this could be a way to share my love of poetry and passion for the plight of the homeless. In my most far-fetched imagination, I would never have expected what happened next.

The following weekend, I was at the beach when I received a text from a poet friend saying, "I'm sorry about the storm that's coming your way." Not knowing what she meant, I responded, "No storm, only beautiful blue skies here." I had no idea a cyclone of opposition to my appointment was gathering strength. I didn't know this position was reserved for poetry elites or that they were enraged. I was unaware the

Governor had deviated from the appointment process they were accustomed to.

After speaking to the first reporter in a telephone interview, it became clear that the media was hostile. The brief information I gave was characterized with a negative slant. Although my poetry had won many awards and had been widely published, I was portrayed as having a "thin resume," and worse. I determined to grant no more interviews. Reporters hounded me at work, at home, and by e-mail, asking incendiary questions.

Soon I was the subject of an ugly social-media storm. I turned on the TV and saw an unflattering picture of me on the screen and news anchors talking about me. Reporters parked outside my house. Friends in far flung states called saying they read about the controversy in their local newspapers. Relatives in New York called to say I was on the front page of their morning papers. I was flooded with letters from all over the U.S. I was shocked to receive messages from poets in other countries. I even ended up in Wikipedia in a negatively slanted article.

I knew I would come out the other side of this cyclone unscathed. My faith in God's good purpose in all that happens encouraged and guided me. I determined not to respond with the same vitriol as my attackers and not to ingest their poison. My husband screened all letters that came to our home, trashing the negative ones. I avoided the TV, stayed off the internet, and never read any of the malevolent blogs. I delighted in the supportive letters I received and many individuals and book clubs requesting my books. I answered every encouraging letter and e-mail, immediately deleting the negative. I was happy to hear from people who said they had never thought much about poetry before, but now decided to read it and even try writing it. People sent me their poems. Others asked me to come to their venues to read my poetry.

Short of two weeks into this storm, I decided the rhetoric of the angry naysayers was not consistent with the positive goals of poetry in my life, and was harmful to poetry as an art form. So, I decided to resign from the position. I wrote a letter of resignation, which was published in newspapers across the country. It read, in part: I remain passionate about the mission of poetry to touch all people regardless of age, education, or social status. I would like to encourage everyone to read and write poetry. They do not need a list of prestigious publishing credits or a collection of accolades from impressive organizations—just the joy of words and appreciation of self-expression.

Little did I know how prophetic my response to my friend's text would be: "No storm, only beautiful blue skies here." I continue to write, share and teach poetry to ordinary people. Proceeds from my second book, *Sleeping Rough*, are donated to the garden I started to feed the homeless. This garden provides over two tons of vegetables per season to people in need. My fourth and most recent book of poetry is *The Shape of Today*, its theme inspired by a quote from Emily Dickinson: To live is so startling it leaves little time for anything else. •

Valerie Macon lives in Fuqua-Varina, North Carolina. Her poetry enlivens the ordinary, paints life fresh. She shares her poems widely in diverse venues, recently included in Kakalak and in Vision and Voice. Her books of poetry are *Shelf Life*, *Sleeping Rough*, *A String of Black Pearls*, and *The Shape of Today*. Currently, she teaches seniors to look for poetry everywhere.

Aunt Jessie

by Vicki Easterly

A unt Jessie lived her adult life within a one-mile radius—half a mile to the east to the garment factory where she worked, half a mile to the west to the church where she worshipped. When she was a little girl, she escaped the drudgery of her farm life by walking to the one-room school down by Flat Creek, where she drank in learning and handfuls of clear water. Her dream was to win the eighth-grade spelling bee. Her mother, Myrtle, helped her study words every night by the kerosene light. But then came the flu epidemic of 1917; Myrtle died on Christmas Eve. With the loss of her mother came the loss of her dream.

Aunt Jessie's baby brother, Roy, was sent up the road to be raised by neighbors, which was the custom in 1917. Jessie, being the oldest at age 12, had to quit school to raise her two-year-old brother, Russell, my daddy. So, she never got to be a child. She never really got to be an adult either. Her father disapproved of his daughters getting married, so Aunt Jessie never left home. As I remember, Aunt Jessie had always seemed content—baking, sewing, reading her Bible. Yet she always wore lipstick, shiny brooches and earrings, and perfume.

Aunt Jessie

Something else stirred within her, I suppose. She was proud of her hip-length hair, braided and wreathed around her head like a halo—a halo she most certainly deserved.

Jessie lived with my granddaddy in a white, clapboard house with a brick-walled front porch. She planted geraniums in concrete flower boxes. She sat alone on the swing in the stifling heat, waving her church fan with the picture of an angel on one side and the funeral home on the other. When my sister, Debbie, and I visited, she made us orange Kool-Aid, and she swung with us.

Living through the Great Depression, Aunt Jessie had learned to salvage everything, including used coffee, which she stored in Mason jars for days. Daddy never knew this, but when he came home on military leave, she served him sugar in his coffee, then saved what was left in the bottom of the cup until it dried so she could use it again. She kept a button box under her bed. She would retrieve it and teach us to thread a needle and to sew buttons onto quilt scraps. Some days, she let us play in her mysterious attic, where she stored "scary things" covered in sheets. At Christmas, she gave us a piece of Juicy Fruit gum, wrapped in a dollar bill. In 1964, I won the seventh-grade spelling bee. Her dream finally came true through me, I suppose. Still, I was sad; I knew how badly she had wanted to win that spelling bee herself so long ago. But she must have felt differently; that day she gave me five dollars!

Daddy loved her like the "mother" she was to him. She loved us like the grandkids she never had. She called us her "dandies."

One day, Aunt Jessie began to cough up blood. The doctor said it was lung cancer. That was so unfair; she never smoked. When she died in 1986, she left behind only her 50-year church pin, a few brooches and some photos in a crumbling black-paged album tied together with a shoelace. One afternoon at the kitchen table, I was flipping carefully through the tattered pages. If the light had not reflected just a certain way, I would never have noticed it. Written in pencil next to a picture of a dapper young man leaning against a gate were the words, "My dearest Charlie." Another page showed the two of them standing together smiling, she in a loose-fitting handkerchief dress, he in jodhpurs. In the margin, she had penciled, "Happier times." The last entry I could make out read simply, "April 14, 1941, Monday. All alone again." I cried.

My sister Debbie pointed out that Aunt Jessie had not always been so content. One picture after the "Charlie" times showed her scowling; in later pictures, her eyes looked dead. Then gradually, pictures showed a transformation until her face had softened into a sweet serenity. At some point, she had totally surrendered to granddaddy and Jesus Christ.

I wondered, did she give up on Charlie, or did Charlie give up on her? Did he marry another girl? Did he carry a faded picture of Jessie? Did he go to war? Did he die? I wish they could have stayed together. I wish she had surrendered to Charlie too. •

Vicki Easterly lives in Frankfort, Kentucky, where she is a member of the Capitol City Writers Roundtable. She has been writing for pleasure since high school. Her short story, "Hallie Holcomb's Hollow," has been published by Carnegie Press. She recently published her first book, *Miracles in the Mundane*. Currently, she is working on poetry and a children's book.

Independence Day, 1968
by Jim Billman

It was the Fourth of July in 1968. The day of the week had no meaning; they were all the same. It was the days we had left that were significant because each new day meant one less day in Vietnam. On this particular Fourth, we had walked a good portion of the day hunting in the jungle of the Central Highlands with a simple mission: to seek and destroy our enemy. Just like yesterday was, and just like tomorrow would be, if …

The heat of the day had taken its toll on the energy reserves of everyone in the rifle company and we hoped that the order to stand-down for the night would soon be issued. Although out of direct sunlight beneath the tree canopy, the floor of the jungle steamed with a humidity that made it difficult to breathe. The need for stealth made movement slow as we made our way up and down the many slippery, root-laden trails the North Vietnamese had previously carved in moving their forces and materials. The foliage was so thick to the sides of the trail that movement there was contrary to our purpose—surprise. It was only when we came to areas defoliated by Agent Orange that we double-timed. We did not want to ever be caught in the open.

But, once a "grunt," an infantryman, understood the jungle, it became an ally of sorts. We listened for sounds and their absences, watched for signs of recent troop movement, and learned what to avoid. A tree was always there to conceal us when we ambushed, and contrary to what one might think, creepy, crawly wildlife was not in abundance. Our problem was the enemy. Each side in this sector of the war zone had the respect of the other as we antagonistically maneuvered to gain the upper hand despite the lack of territorial rights of domain. We had more technology, but they had more know-how and the home-field advantage. The only thing we had in common was how we bled.

This mission had kept us out for over 20 days of what would become 40. Resupplied by air drops and supported by artillery fire bases, we carried our weapons at the ready and everything else on our backs as we moved from one nameless hill to another. I was a lieutenant, the "target of priority" recognizable by the soldier with a radio and antenna on his back who followed me. As the second-in-command for the Company, I had the responsibility of knowing our location so we could call for artillery support that could be the deciding factor in a firefight. That's why my platoon often found itself to be the one walking point.

It was not the best of times. I was grimy from crossing muddy hills, filthy from not having showered or changed clothes for twenty-some days, sore from the weight of my pack, and I still had nearly 300 days left in country. Furthermore, the day before had been my first wedding anniversary. Now, years hence, I remember this Fourth of July evening not for the battle we waged or the casualties we inflicted, but for the emotion it evoked.

Night comes fast in the tropics. We had set up ambush positions to a side of the trail when just after dark, we saw flashes in the distance maybe five "clicks" away. Thinking this was an air strike and immediately wondering what the implications might be, we watched. It didn't take long to realize that these flashes were not incendiary explosives, but fireworks being launched from a nearby firebase. It was our Independence Day celebration half a world away that made the sky brilliant for all to see. For about an hour I wanted to think the war came to a halt as two ideological extremes came together as a single group of people enjoying the view.

The fireworks didn't alleviate our situation or enhance our relationship with the enemy, but they reminded me that there is a common link to all mankind: we share the sky, the air, and the earth. To me, the display suggested there was a way out, a plane home, an end to the destruction of a land and people that I found beautiful, and closure for a war I did not understand.

Now, 50 years later, a Fourth of July never passes that I do not reflect on that time as one of the defining moments of my life. I learned that no matter how bleak the situation, how miserable the conditions, or how minimal the options, there's often a tiny, sometimes unrelated spark of light that can help us get through our darkest days. •

Independence Day, 1968

Jim Billman lives in Owensboro, Kentucky, and has been a soldier, an educator, and the owner of a small construction business. Now devoting much of his time to writing, he has authored a non-fiction book about public school reform and a historical mystery novel. His present work is a coming-of-age novel about a young man who moves from a rural school to an inner-city one.

Following in Dad's Footsteps
by Eliza Strickland

M y father's father was a contractor. When Dad was in college, he worked a couple of summers for my grandfather on construction sites scattered across the hills and hollows in and around Floyd County, Kentucky, the place they both grew up. Our ancestors had come there to the Big Sandy Valley, legend had it, with none other than Daniel Boone himself.

Those summers, to hear Dad tell it, he was humping concrete blocks around from one end of a site to the other, all day, every day.

I asked him once, not long ago, "How did you know you wanted to be a lawyer? Did you ever want to go into construction like your dad?" And in response, somewhat sheepishly, he told me about those summers, and he said: "I knew after that that I needed a job where I didn't have to haul things around all day long. The physical exhaustion was incredible. I would just go home and go to sleep, and I would dream about it at night, and then I had to wake up at the crack of dawn and do it again.

"And I knew then I'd better get a good degree, because I knew I couldn't do that."

It happens this way, maybe more often than we think, that the way you end up doing one thing is because you know you can't do something else. We have to make do with who we are. Once we figure out who that is.

Some forty years after my dad made his concrete-block-induced discovery in eastern Kentucky, I had my own concrete-block summer—though for me it was spread out over a couple of years.

Following Dad's blueprint for a successful career, I had become a lawyer and was working at a law firm in Washington, D.C. But eventually, carrying the weight of all the hard-to-define elements of a fast-paced legal career took a toll. I had the realization, *I couldn't do that.*

I left my job at the firm, and tried a different, non-lawyer job, and then left that too, and had a child, and put all my resources into taking care of her. I was happy doing what I was doing, but I was still feeling like a failure in some ways, like I had let Dad down, by leaving law.

It was then that I thought to ask him how he knew he wanted to be a lawyer in the first place. It had never occurred to me that Dad might once have felt the same way I did, that he might have feared he had failed, or let his father down, by becoming a *lawyer.*

But here he was telling me that he went to law school because he *had* to, because he knew that he could not do the other jobs he would have had to do otherwise. Almost as if becoming a lawyer was a cop-out.

I started to wonder if perhaps my own "failure" wasn't inherent to me, as I had assumed it was. What if I was on a path that had been trod before me by my father, and before us by any number of parents and children?

We had ended up in different places, Dad and I. But the impulse that led us there was the same. He, too, had discovered he had to make do with who he was, with what he knew he could do. And if he could turn that into a success story, then maybe I could too.

Years before Daniel Boone led my ancestors to the land that they would make their home, he made what some might call a disastrous first foray into Kentucky. In what would become Floyd County, Boone and his party had followed a well-trod buffalo path to a salt lick, when an early snowstorm caught them off guard. Running low on supplies, they decided to camp there through the long winter.

Boone made do with where he was and with what he had, and he lived to tell the tale. His path did not end at the salt lick, though I wonder if he feared—at least for a while—that it would. After that expedition, he made many return trips to Kentucky that helped make him a legend, each time building on his hard-won knowledge.

Maybe, after all, it isn't a failure to camp by the salt lick and wait out the winter, shooting what comes your way instead of forging out in search of it. Maybe that's just smart use of resources.

Maybe there is worth in making do—with what's around us, with who we are. And maybe, paradoxically, once we learn to make do with what we have, the path broadens with possibility. •

Eliza Kendrick Strickland now lives in Durham, North Carolina. She grew up in eastern Kentucky, the ninth generation of her father's family to make a home there. After studying creative writing at UNC-Chapel Hill, Eliza earned a J.D. and an LL.M. at Duke. She now writes essays and fiction. This year, Eliza's father will retire after 42 years of practicing law.

Earning the Badge

by Deborah Wilson

"Nobody limps across my stage," First Sergeant Keyes said. My boots, as reflective as a mirror, lined with moleskin with added support for the arches, had been described as a hotel for feet. A little Achilles pain was not going to stop me. In dress uniform, I now joined the graduating class of 1975 as I received my Drill Sergeant Badge.

I always said my husband "drafted" me into the Army. In 1974, the Army offered two-week Basic Training to women bringing civilian acquired skills into the Reserves. Added incentives included advanced pay rate plus automatic promotion. I enlisted, completed Basic Training, and returned to the 91st Division Training Unit as a clerk.

Soon after my promotion to Specialist, the 91st Division started its own Leadership Academy, a Drill Sergeant School. Sent to the Academy as its clerk, I asked the commandant, "Do they ever let women take the class?"

"Take a seat." That wasn't exactly what I meant. I had just finished Basic Training. What did I know? These were all combat veterans, including my husband. The oldest was a forty-nine-year-old logger from Washington who was about to run circles around everybody else. I was a housewife in my everyday life.

I maintained fitness between monthly Reserve drills with karate. The downtown studio was owned by Mike Orlando, a mustached, former bouncer, with shag-cut black hair. The motto, "You only fail if you quit trying," hung on a plaque outside his office. The contract included a private lesson plus two group lessons per week. With a quick assessment as to my purpose, I became the only woman in the men's class. As I became stronger and more flexible, Mr. Orlando used me as the sweat barometer gauging the effectiveness of his classes. While it is true that men are generally stronger, I was not about to mention they also tend to perspire sooner than women, and that women tend to be more flexible. Mr. Orlando chided anybody who acted the gentleman and did not try to punch me. He would stand behind me, locking my horse stance so I had no choice but to defend myself.

Although my hair had been short throughout childhood, my husband loved my hair long. Fine tresses have a mind of their own. The Army won the argument. My hair was cut according to regulation, but not so short as to present a manly appearance. I missed my long locks as much as my husband did.

Each drill weekend meant another selection for the leadership position. I seemed to be picked every other month. "Make those windows rattle." Command voice and presence had to be developed for cadence to be heard by a company of recruits.

Specific methods of training were taught, leadership traits memorized, and counseling skills practiced.

Eventually, it was time for the final two weeks of active duty training at Fort Ord. It is not the leader's responsibility to know or do everything, but to complete the mission. That was how I handled the leadership confidence course. Why not use an engineer's knowledge? I had an engineer on my team.

Great emphasis was placed on proper protocol during counseling, especially when dealing with members of the opposite sex. Apparently one instructor did not get the message. I easily parried his unwanted advances while looking toward the opposite end of the bleachers. Classmates had discreetly moved closer to my husband. Those behind and beside him restrained him by holding his belt. Those in front pressed against his legs as fury colored his face. We were constantly graded on military bearing.

As the weekend neared, selection was made for company commander, "Sgt. Wilson." My husband stepped forward.

"Not that Sgt. Wilson." I was again under the microscope. It was the day we were running the ranges, in an age when weapon training was not part of women's Basic Training. While everybody else enjoyed breaks, I learned how to fire a rifle. I earned initiative points by falling behind the class to stand at the back of the room to observe what was happening.

Training came to an end. As far as I know, my husband and I became the first husband-wife drill sergeant team in the Army

Reserves. We returned to our home unit together.

That was not the end of the challenge. Annual training for 1976 was at Fort Leonard Wood, Missouri. The Commanding General was incensed to discover a qualified drill sergeant hidden in the typing pool when all were needed on the field.

Morning dawned for the 10-mile forced march. My tall husband led while I had the tail. Male egos dared not drop out as they saw a woman keeping pace behind them.

"Why aren't you sweating?" active-duty counterparts asked. •

Born in front of her grandmother's Texas home, Deborah C. Wilson is the seventh of nine children. She has traveled like everybody in her mostly military family and takes inspiration from her adventures. Deborah now lives in Winston-Salem, North Carolina. She is a member of Winston-Salem Writers.

Rainbows, Clouds, and Promises

by Catherine Rhoden-Goguen

The sound of rain has a serene effect on me, much like a warm towel fresh out of the dryer, a handmade quilt on a wintry day, or the glow from a fireplace and the aroma of burning logs. Some things just always seem to warm the soul. When I was younger, I remember my Dad going out to the car, just so he could hear the rain pour down on a "tin" roof, for as with me, the rain resonated with his soul. And that's how I grew up. My Dad and I watched clouds together and we chose the ones we wanted to take a ride on and speculated on where we'd end up. We were both so in tune with nature—two peas in a pod.

But childhood ends; we can't stay in such idyllic comfort. However, I clung to reminders of it and maintained a childlike awe of my father, who I continue to think hung the moon.

As often is the case after we grow up, I moved away, but I always wished childhood and adulthood could be combined. In 2017, my wish came true. My parents decided to move from their home, a house my grandfather and dad had built together, to an apartment near me.

On the day of the move, I awoke to unwanted rain, and I drove to the apartment to wait on the moving van and my parents both en route. The Weather Channel predicted all-day rain, but as I glanced up from my phone, I saw a beautiful rainbow arc across the apartment building. The rain had suddenly stopped. That rainbow was a promise as old as biblical times that all was going to be okay; and, it was ... until three weeks later.

Imagine you arrive at the hospital to find the person you love most in the world has died.

"Your father took a sudden turn and passed away shortly before you arrived."

The emotions are so overwhelming and tortuous. One wonders how the body and spirit can survive, but somehow, we do. Then, imagine after that devastating news, you are told, "There's been a mix up" while you are simultaneously seeing your Dad being wheeled from the opposite end of the hallway towards you ... like a ghost.

My mind could not process the confusion; and, no one from the nursing staff stuck around to explain. It was as if they had only said, "We've left lettuce off your cheeseburger. Here it is. Sorry." I rushed to my Dad sobbing; I held him close. I was on an emotional rollercoaster: joy, grief, shock, and then anger—anger as I realized someday I would have to experience his death all over again. To suffer this loss twice. How could I possibly do so?

I spent the rest of the day with my Dad. I left the hospital in Corbin, Kentucky, feeling overwhelmed. I was unforgiving of the incompetence that had caused me the deepest grief I had ever known. This was not a case of my Dad almost dying and being resuscitated. This was a case where a team of health care workers had mixed up the patients.

At home, I was happy to see my bed, to de-stress and to hope that I could find some peace. Sleep did not come easily, but it came … until the jangle of my phone awoke me at 5:00 a.m.

> "Your father has become bradycardic and we need you to come to the hospital."

> "Are you sure it's my Dad? Yesterday you told me he was dead."

> "He told me about driving you on choir trips …."
> My heart sank.

> "Is he in ICU?"

> "He has a DNR so we can't do anything."

> "My father does not have a DNR. Take him to ICU immediately! For God's sake, do something!"

As I listen to the rain now, I think back to that rainbow and the promise it made to me and then broke. My Dad died … alone. He had not signed an order for "Do Not Resuscitate."

Rainbows, Clouds, and Promises

He had walked into the hospital with abdominal pain. He was not supposed to die. How could so much go so wrong in two short days? I fear I will never know because, sadly, it seems hospitals are more concerned with lawsuits than with telling patients what they did.

Doctors deliver us at birth, so it seems almost instinctual to trust them, but that blind trust is destroyed. I now question everything I once believed. Just the sight of a rainbow makes my heart scream, *Liar*!

For now, the rain allows me to suspend disbelief long enough to feel the presence of my Dad. My tears fall, and my soul resonates with the downpour. I whisper, "I love you, Daddy." •

Catherine Rhoden-Goguen resides in Barbourville, Kentucky, where she is a retired teacher and playwright. Her play, *May I Have Your Attention Please?*, published by Pioneer Drama, Englewood, Colorado, has been performed all over the U.S. and Canada and in Great Britain and Ireland. The play won the prestigious *Critic's Choice Award* at the Wisconsin State Theatre Festival.

Smack That Azz

by J'Lissabeth Faughn

I'm nervous speaking with my supervisor. Am I overreacting?

I haven't done anything wrong, but I don't feel good. I am uncomfortable. I feel dirty.

I think.

Maybe that's not it. I don't think I know what feeling dirty feels like beyond the literal.

"So, what's bothering you J'Lissabeth?" he says with generosity and a Cheshire grin.

My Southern mother advised her children never to stir the pot.

I take a deep breath. "I want to talk to you about Joe Jackson."

"You mean Michael's father or the maintenance supervisor?" he jokes.

I get it. He realizes I'm nervous and he's making jokes to put me at ease. I want him to freaking stop. I need him to listen. I will play along.

Smack That Azz

"Well of course it's about Michael Jackson and his father," I chuckle. "With Michael's recent passing, I am concerned about who is going to get custody of his pet chimp Bubbles. I don't think Joe will provide the necessary environment for him to thrive."

He looks confused at my response, so I raise my hands. "Just forget it. Bad joke. It's about my maintenance supervisor."

I oversee an area of campus housing at a large university.

"The day after our first area meeting Joe came up to me and said, 'You know often we don't get big ole' girls like you. I like big white girls.' I just replied, 'Uuh huh' and kept walking. I didn't really know how to respond. A few days later, he approached me and said, 'You know a lot us black men like big white women. Particularly big white girls with blonde hair' and he twirled his finger around in my hair. I said, 'Yes. I'm aware that is a fetish many men have' and I walked away."

OK, why has the grin not evaporated from his face?

He gestures for me to continue.

"About a week later, I was leaving my office to do Bikram yoga with Mohammad—"

"Oh, how was that?" he interjects.

"Um . . . it was horrible?" Has he heard a word I've said? I'm tired of looking at his teeth. "I don't know why I thought doing Yoga in 105- degree heat would be any more fun than doing it at a normal temperature—"

"Yeah, I thought about doing it, but I don't like heat," he interupts.

I must have a perplexed look on my face because the damn smile on his face finally fades. "I'm sorry Jizzy," he says. "Go ahead."

I hate the nickname Jizzy. It's obscene to me. I've told my colleagues I don't like it. I feel like leaving. But I don't.

I tell him about the day I was going to yoga. How Joe yelled "Oh wow! Look at that nice big pumpkin ass" as I left my office. A few days later he began yelling, "I'm waiting to smack that ass," which he has continued shouting this past week every time he sees me.

"I don't really know what to say," I'm finishing. "I know I should tell Joe to stop. But I've never had a man hit on me. As J'Lissabeth. As a woman."

"Oh wow, that's GREAT Jizzy!" my boss giggles. "Thank you for sharing."

I am confused.

"Can you imagine how Joe would even begin to process that you are not a real woman?" He is laughing. "If he knew you were a transwoman . . ."

I begin to fade out. I'm perturbed and perplexed.

I'm feeling harassed by Joe.

This. *Oh, my God.* THIS is what sexual harassment is.

Smack That Azz

This is what women feel when men harass them.

My boss didn't listen to me.

I feel like my body is moving but I'm not in it. I'm walking outside away from his office and back to mine.

"Hey, J'lissabeth." I hear my name. A shock runs through me. My face turns red.

I'm back in my body. The voice is coming from my right side. I can see Joe waving at me from about 30 feet away.

"When you gonna let me smack that ass?" he yells. I hear several passing students laugh.

Shame on me for doing whatever it is I have done to encourage this behavior.

Shame on me for not confronting him.

Shame on me. •

J'Lissabeth Faughn majored in Theatre at Murray State University, completing graduate studies in Education Leadership and Policy Studies (Social Justice) at Iowa State University. In 2017, J'Lissabeth received a grant from the National Society of Arts and Letters (Kentucky Chapter). She graduated from the Author's Academy at the Carnegie Center for Literacy and Learning in Lexington, Kentucky, where she lives.

Divine Guidance

by Judie Holcomb-Pack

I believe that God has influenced decisions I've made that led me one way when I could have so easily gone another. Not that I've seen any burning bushes or visions of the Virgin Mary, or dreams foretelling my future. It's more like being inspired to move in a surprising direction.

Such as the decision to marry my husband.

Being a single mom, few evenings out met my criteria of a "date": (1) must call more than 24 hours in advance; (2) must pick me up at my house; and, (3) must pay for the entire evening. But in the summer of 1989, I found myself actually juggling TWO men. One was an IRS agent who, as I often rated dates, "looked good on paper." He had a job, owned a house, had a dog, and his parents were dead—all positive points when you're sizing up a potential mate. But he was persnickety and possessed one trait that caused me distress: he loved country music.

Now I love all types of music, too. But I grew up on rock-and-roll and beach music and have absolutely no appreciation for country music. One evening he decided to persuade me to change my views, and for two hours he serenaded me with various country songs and artists. When he played the last song, I could take it no more, and I said, "Good Lord, I could write a better song than that!"

"No, you couldn't," he replied.
"Yes, I could."
"No, you couldn't."
"Give me a pencil and paper," I demanded.

And that's when God must have intervened in His infinite wisdom because in a matter of minutes, I had written new words to the music of the song he had just played. The words flowed out of me and onto the paper like molasses on a biscuit.

"There!" I said, and presented him with my country song entitled, "The Alien and the Redneck." It had all the makings of a hit: a pickup truck, a coon dog, and beer. The lyrics captured the pathos of a country boy in an intergalactic mystery:

> I was going down Highway 68
> in my pickup truck with my coon dog, Jake,
> When all of a sudden this light up in the sky
> Came barreling down over the top of me
> and shined so bright I could hardly see
> And I thought for sure that I was gonna die.
>
> Things got quiet, so I looked outside.
> I saw this object and then I spied
> The strangest creatures looking back at me.

They were tall and thin with pointed noses,
long green arms and legs and toes-es
And the darnedest haircut you would ever see.

There was even a haunting refrain:

Mr. Alien, Mr. Alien, don't put your hex on me.
I'm just a good ole' country boy.
Don't put your hex on me.

It could have been made the Top 10 on WTQR. I could visual-
ize a banjo playing backup to the vocals as the story continued
to unfold:

He said they wanted a specimen
of the finest earthling type of man
To compare with them and it was gonna be me.
Well, I felt quite proud – who'd suspect
that an Alabama boy, just a Southern redneck
Would be the one to make space history.

I felt real proud, so I cooperated
and told them how we operated
And described the fine life we all had down here.
I showed them my card from the NRA,
my cowboy boots, then started to play
Some songs by Willie and gave them all a beer.

I never saw creatures drink that way.
They'd guzzle a beer then try to play
Some country songs, but they sounded kinda bland.
The more they drank, the greener they got

'til I thought for sure they were gonna pop
Before they could get that spacecraft home again.

The last stanza was especially touching:

They sobered up about five hours later,
feeling sick as a dog and mean as a 'gator,
And flew me back to where Jake was waiting for me.
And as they were leaving I heard one say,
"Those earthling men are really okay,
But those long-eared women sure ain't much to see."

Surprisingly, the persnickety, country-music-lovin' IRS agent
never called me again. Having eliminated the competition, on
New Year's Eve 1989, I married my husband.

It's only right that I end this story with a little verse:

Was it divine guidance or the hand of fate
That helped me marry the better mate?
Sometimes, I swear that making do
Is seeing what's right in front of you. •

Judie Holcomb-Pack is retired from Winston-Salem's Crisis Control
Ministry. She is editor/writer for "For Seniors Only" magazine. She
won gold medals in Senior Games/SilverArts competitions for poetry and short stories. She serves on the boards of Winston-Salem
Writers and 40 Plus Stage Company. Judie enjoys a great cup of coffee and stimulating conversation; and, she is a die-hard Virginia Tech
Hokies football fan.

Omaha

by Howard Pearre

On the cold beach, they stood crowded inside rectangles drawn in the sand. The rectangles simulated the Higgins landing crafts which would carry them, thirty-two men each. They practiced assembling into the outlines so each man would quickly find his precise spot for the two-hour-long trip. The lieutenant stood at the front of one of the "boats," gave the order, and the imaginary steel ramp was lowered. His men, "pushed" by sergeants in the stern, charged out. Then they practiced actual landings, storming the English coastline.

On June 5, he, along with streams of men loaded down with weapons and equipment, boarded the LST that would carry them most of the way across the Channel. Sleep was not possible, but they found spaces throughout the ship to crouch down and try to get some rest.

H-Hour would be at 0630. He had instructed his men about the hedgehogs, tetrahedrons, and Belgian Gates, obstacles the Germans had deployed in the shallow waters near the beach capable of ripping apart the mostly plywood landing boats. If they made it onto the shore, they knew barbed wire and mines awaited them, making them easy targets for machine gunners looking down from fortified pillboxes. But they also knew that Navy guns and air bombardments would "soften" the beaches before the landing, and that "floating tanks," also deployed from the LSTs, would help clear the beach as they made their way to the protective shelf 200 yards from the water's edge.

In the darkness, the LST lumbered into the deeper waters of the Channel. It was uncomfortable and cramped, but every man knew this was the easy part. Later in the night as the ship was underway, the infantry companies assembled on the deck, and cargo nets were lowered from the ship's side. When the LST reached its designated location, far from the coast of France, the Higgins boats were lowered to the water.

The lieutenant gave the order for his men to climb over the rail, down the cargo netting, and into their boat as they had practiced so many times.

As their landing craft got underway, the noise from its diesel outboard motor was incessant. The propeller, freed from the water whenever the boat pitched forward, screamed. Crashing seas bashed against its sides, and men swayed back and forth, falling on and clutching one another to keep their positions. They swayed and groaned and were seasick. For two hours the boat churned through the Channel.

The order-giver had done it before. His F Company had land-ed in Sicily a year ago. When the fighting was done, the Army had put a Purple Heart and a Silver Star on his chest and had made him a lieutenant. It wasn't a reward for bravery; the First Division was desperate for officers with demonstrated courage.

But as before, he struggled to control his emotions. He was their leader. Without his steady hand, his men would perish, and the mission would be lost. And yet many other thoughts distracted him. He thought about when he was a child growing up in Georgia, seeing Camp Gordon soldiers bound for the trenches of the Great War. He thought about his mother making biscuits in a wood-fired stove and seeing her wiping her hands, dusty with flour, on her apron. He thought about his bossy older sister, a younger version of his mother. He thought about his skinny younger brother who sometimes was the target of bullies, who, in turn, learned that this particular skinny kid had a big brother with fists. His hand went to a chest pocket that held a photograph of Helen, the New York gal with a cocky smile who had captured his heart, in her smart brown wedding day suit. He tried to focus on the business at hand, readying himself for anything—a snag from a submerged hedgehog that would tear a fatal hole in the Higgins, immediate enemy fire as the ramp was lowered.

He did not know just how tragically the day would proceed, that the "softening" bombardments would either completely miss the German armaments or not occur at all because of overcast skies, that almost all of the "floating tanks" would sink in the rough seas, that whipping winds would push the Higgins landing craft directly in front of German fortifications that overlooked the beach, that half his men would be killed minutes after they landed, and that he would never reach the protective shelf.

Omaha

111

Lieutenant Howard E. Pearre prayed he'd have the courage to do his job that day—courage, simply choosing by will alone to do what must be done.

He knew he'd already chosen. •

Howard Pearre retired in 2015 after a career as a counselor and manager with NC Vocational Rehabilitation and the Veterans Administration. He lives in Winston-Salem, North Carolina, where he is a member of Winston-Salem Writers. His short fiction pieces have appeared in Second Spring and Silver Arts publications. He has six grandchildren, avoids Saturday crossword puzzles, and makes fig wine.

Civil War Hard Times
by Betsy Burch

It was the fall of 1862 and times were difficult to bear. The U.S. Civil War was being fought over states' rights, the expansion of slavery, and other matters. It was especially hard living here in Kentucky because many families were divided as to whether to fight for the North or the South, for the Union or for the Confederacy. Brothers fought against brothers and sons against fathers. The governor of Kentucky was pro-Confederate, but soldiers raised for the defense of Kentucky were divided between the pro-Southern State Guard and the pro-Union Home Guard.

Here, in central Kentucky, my great-great-grandmother, Sally, was having a difficult time keeping hearth and home together. She, like many other mothers, was raising her children alone because her husband was off fighting the war. My great-great-grandfather, James, had just left home almost a month before to return to his regiment. He had been home on furlough for the birth of their third child. Then there was the awful Battle of Richmond fought just a few miles down the road; her husband's regiment had not been involved in it. This was a blessing to Sally because so many had died in that 2-day battle.

In truth, James belonged to two regiments. Whichever unit he was with at any given time depended upon whether he had a horse. In October 1861, he enlisted and was mustered into Company K, 1st Kentucky Volunteer Cavalry under Colonel Frank Lane Wolford. In January1862, he attached himself to the Union 20th Kentucky Infantry. The two units were sometimes together; and, from time to time, the muster rolls showed him in one or the other.

In Kentucky, a drought had persisted for many months; livestock was dying because of starvation and dehydration. To add to these problems, the weather was extremely hot—100 degrees in the shade. All these things were devastating to the economy of Madison County, an agricultural community. Sally found herself mired in all the difficulties on a personal level; her milk cow was close to death from starvation and her kitchen garden had stopped producing vegetables for lack of water. The economy of her household was now at risk because her cow could no longer produce; Sally could no longer churn cream to make butter she could sell or barter. Her chickens were still doing fairly well, so she continued to sell eggs to help her household funds.

Sally's oldest daughter, Ann, was six years old, but already quite helpful in caring for her siblings: John, my great-grandfather, who was three, and Rosa, two months of age.

Over the next several months, Sally continued to live day by day as best she could by sheer grit and determination. After all, this was the right thing to do. She heard only snippets of information from neighbors. Neither she nor James could read or write, so direct communication was out of the question. Several men from their neighborhood of Poosey Ridge had enlisted when James had done so. The news coming back home was that there was a rivalry ensuing between Union Cavalry Colonel Wolford and Confederate Cavalry General John Hunt Morgan. The regiments James was in were noted to be at Camp Wildcat and Mills Springs in southern Kentucky, at Louisville and Perryville, and at Lebanon, Tennessee (near Nashville).

In late 1863, Sally received news that James had been in action on October 20th at Philadelphia, Tennessee, in a cavalry skirmish. Philadelphia was a small market town; it had a railroad bridge over the Tennessee River that was a strategic prize for the Union forces. And, it was the southernmost Union-held town at that time. Two Confederate cavalry brigades approached Philadelphia from the south and surprised Wolford's men. The Confederates violated a flag of truce in this action, which marked the first defeat of the Union forces during the occupation of eastern Tennessee. Twenty-five soldiers were wounded, and 447 were captured. In this "rout" of the Union, seven of Wolford's men were killed—including my great-great-grandfather. His death occurred two years to the day after his initial enlistment.

Sally also received information that her husband had been listed as absent without leave and as a deserter; but, she knew James was not the type of man to shirk his responsibilities. He believed wholeheartedly in his place in the conflict, the battle between the North and the South. She also knew that a soldier leaving his regiment with or without leave in the Civil War (as well as during the Revolutionary War) did not mean much. Soldiers would take leave to go home to bring in a crop, for the birth of a child, or for other reasons.

In 1880, Sally filed for a Civil War Widow's Pension. It had taken many years for the muster rolls and casualty sheets of the two regiments, cavalry and infantry, to come together. A notation from the Adjutant General's Office dated January 4, 1886, stated the charge against James—the charge of desertion—was removed.

Twenty-three years after her husband's death during the Civil War, Sally received her pension. It had been said of Sally that "she was the meanest woman in Madison County until she got her pension." Sally then purchased property on Taylor's Fork in Madison County and moved her family there, where they continued to grow and have their own families, descendants of Kentucky stalwarts, the brave and persistent James and Sally Murphy. •

Elizabeth M. (Betsy) Burch, a mother of three sons and a grandmother, lives in Richmond, Kentucky. She is Past Regent of the Boonesborough Chapter, Daughters of the American Revolution, with an avid interest in history and genealogy. After retiring from oncology nursing, she began writing her personal stories including her experiences during four years at a girls' boarding school.

Calm Down

by Suzanne Cottrell

Today I would take my first solo flight. I felt like a ball of tightly bound rubber bands ready to pop. The traffic pattern altitude for the Knightdale Airport was 1,313 feet, so I had almost two hundred feet to spare with the current cloud ceiling at 1,500 feet. I had to fly below the clouds to maintain ground visibility as I was not yet certified for instrument flying.

I diligently went through my Cessna-150-single-engine-pre-flight-inspection checklist. For my solo check off, I had to fly the pattern just once and land safely. Having visually scanned to make sure the area around the propeller was clear, I shouted, "Clear." I felt a bit lonely as the plane hastened down the runway.

Here I go, as I pulled back on the yoke. The nose angled upward and cut through the air like a warm knife through butter. All I could see was blue sky as the plane ascended. Eventually, I trimmed the elevators, leveled off, and cut the fuel mixture back to lean. I was ready to cruise and to enjoy my freedom. I began to bank to the left and start the crosswind segment of the flight pattern. That's when I noticed wisps of clouds in my peripheral vision.

Where did they come from? I'm only at 800 feet.

My left leg began to twitch, then to shake. Fluffy, white clouds drifted toward me. I had to react quickly to maintain visibility of the airport.

Don't panic.

My mouth became dry. My leg was trembling so vigorously that I had to push down with my left hand, trying to steady it. I wished I could nail it in place, never mind the pain.

Calm down, you've got this. My muscles tightened. My teeth clenched. My eyes focused intently on the airport.

I banked hard to the left. Now I was flying parallel to the runway, less than a mile from the airport. Once I was past the end of the runway, I could turn onto the base leg and then turn once more to make my final approach. I had to keep the airport and runway in view and get down fast. As I approached the runway, the tree tops grew uncomfortably close. I imagined my feet scrapping across the tree tops. I mumbled a brief prayer. I tried to replay my instructor's emergency procedures in my head. I never thought I'd have to use them.

There'd better not be any cows on the runway.

I'd heard that pilots frequently had to buzz the rural runway to scare the cows off before they could make their final approach.

Not today, please, no cows today.

I knew I was coming in too fast, but if I pulled back on the throttle too quickly, I could stall the engine and I was already too low. I could crash into tree tops or become a metal heap on the runway.

Snap out of it. Get control. Full flaps.

My airspeed dropped to 65 knots, still too fast.

Steady, ease back on the throttle.

The wheels walloped the asphalt. Wham! The plane bounced up, and I felt like I was a yo-yo on a string. The wheels struck the pavement again, jolting my body. Thankfully, the plane stayed down on the runway this time.

Whew, that was close. Hold on.

My feet pumped the pedals as the plane rumbled down the runway at what felt like lightning speed.

"Stop, stop!" I was talking to the plane now.

I kept talking to myself trying to control the plane. When it came to a screeching halt at the end of the runway, my heart was pounding and my whole body was quivering. The smell of burnt rubber disgusted me, yet I was so relieved to be back on the ground in one piece. Blood flowed back into my whitened knuckles.

"Brakes on, check."

I clambered out of the plane. My knees buckled. I braced myself against a wing strut to regain my composure.

Calm Down

Eventually, I made my way to the office.

The office manager looked up. "Congratulations," he said. "You did it, your first solo flight. You ready to go up again?"

"Go again!" I exclaimed. I was incredulous. "I was told the ceiling was 1,500 feet. No way! I had clouds rolling in at 800. It's a miracle I got back."

"Calm down. You made it," he reminded me. "Your instructor will be real proud of you."

I know the office manager was just trying to reassure me, but his words were not much consolation. I was too upset to appreciate my accomplishment. I would fly another day, but I did not intend to take any chances with the visibility. Perhaps getting my instrument rating would not be a bad idea after all.•

Copyright 2018, Suzanne Cottrell

Suzanne Cottrell, a member of the Granville Writers' Group and NC Writers' Network, lives with her husband and three rescue dogs in Granville County, North Carolina. An outdoor enthusiast and retired teacher, she enjoys reading, writing, hiking, and Pilates. Her work has appeared in numerous journals and anthologies, including *Pop Machine*, *Unwanted Visitors*, *Women's Voices*, *Parks and Points*, and *Nailpolish Stories*.

Uncle Carlton

by Beth Bixby Davis

"Don't worry, Mommy, I'm okay." These were the welcome words that awakened my grandmother late that cold November night in 1932. Heartbroken to the core and grief-stricken beyond comprehension, she needed this assurance to bolster her strong faith in the existence of the hereafter.

Carlton, almost 13, was the youngest of the three children in my father's family, born December 21, 1919. My grandparents ran the dairy farm that had been in the family since 1838. It was a self-sufficient farm where everyone worked hard to take care of the three dozen dairy cattle, the pigs, chickens and work horses. They raised their own vegetables, grew the hay and grain for the animals, cut their own wood for heat and provided a loving, stable home for their children. They had no indoor plumbing or electricity until my dad was a teenager. Church was important to them, and they attended the local Methodist church each week. In the winter when their car was up on blocks, they traveled to church either by horse-and-buggy or horse-and-sleigh, depending on the condition of the roads.

Uncle Carlton

121

A handsome and happy young man, Carlton loved animals; he did well in school and was adored by his parents and older brother and sister. As a very young boy, he used to trap mice for a penny each and he kept books to track his earnings. At one time, he offered to give my dad, who was seven years older, all his earnings to help with my dad's college expenses. Carlton thought that later when my dad was a successful veterinarian he could then help him go to college. A kind and generous spirit was my Uncle Carlton. My dad, a sophomore at Cornell in 1932, had promised to bring Carlton a pet guinea pig the next time he came home.

One Sunday morning Carlton and his dad (my grandfather) went partridge hunting. They did this often, and they loved getting their shotguns and taking a break from the hard work at the farm. Carlton was opposite his dad, on the other side of a bunch of cedars and out of sight, when my grandfather shot at a flying bird. A pellet went through the trees and hit Carlton in the eye. My grandfather carried him out of the field and somehow got him to the hospital. His son, Carlton, died that same day. It was November 6, 1932.

I never knew my Uncle Carlton, of course; and when I think of this incident, my thoughts are with my grandfather who never got over the tragic accident that took the life of his beloved youngest son. The family worried about my grandfather a great deal until his death in 1946. He would often take long walks in the woods, always wanting to be alone. Exactly one year after the tragedy, being deeply distracted, my grandfather had an accident in his sawmill resulting in the partial loss of his hand.

And, I often think of my strong, brave grandmother who, while in the depths of the worst grieving one can imagine, was also trying her best to comfort her heartbroken and guilt-ridden husband. She spent hours and days controlling her own grief trying to help my grandfather.

In a journal of family history, my dad told the story of getting the phone call at Cornell from Ralph, a close friend of the family.

> Ralph said, "Donald."
> "Yes."
> He said, "Brace yourself, I have very bad news."
> "What?"
> He said, "Your father shot Carlton; he is dead. It was an accident."
> "I will be home, but have to see what arrangements I can make."

He took a bus to Syracuse and was picked up by family friends. It was a long ride home as they explained all they knew about it and repeatedly said it was an accident. Dad said, "I don't know what they were thinking, because I never doubted for a second but that it was an accident."

My dad fully intended to stay home and to help his parents all he could, but they would not allow it. This rural farm family had deep faith, which I'm certain was what got them through these terrible times. My grandmother lived until 1985, when she died at age 97, having been a widow for 39 years. I'd like to

Uncle Carlton

think that Carlton's words to her on that sad November night in 1932—"Don't worry, Mommy, I'm okay"—comforted her during many long days and nights. I never asked my grandmother about Carlton, but I wish I had. I believe she might have liked very much to tell me about her son. •

Beth Bixby Davis was born in Northern New York and moved to the Asheville area of North Carolina in the mid-1960s where she reared her family, raised Arabian horses, and had a 30-year career in nursing. Enjoying a long-time hobby of writing essays and poetry, she recently took a class in flash fiction. She belongs to Talespinners Writers Group.

The Water Always Wins
by Cheryl Powell

There she was sitting on a lawn chair, chin in her hands, a mother out of solutions. Three little kids toddled around the yard, unaware that their home was being filled with dirty water rising from the little creek behind. It was the summer of 1969 and we knew exactly how she felt.

One year prior, Laurie, Bev, and I were deep asleep in that same house on a lazy summer morning. Mom came stomping up the stairs to my attic bedroom, strongly grabbed my shoulder and started rocking me back and forth, telling me to get up. Stuck in my deep, teenage sleep I didn't realize the urgency until she started yelling.

"The house is flooding! The creek's rising and it's still pouring rain. It'll soon be up to the door. We gotta get out of here!" I couldn't imagine that little trickle of a creek down in that deep, deep hole behind our house could become such a threat. I assumed Mom was in a state of hysteria. She had been prone to this ever since we left Pennsylvania last summer and moved to the suburbs of Cleveland, Ohio. I rolled out to see what the hell she was talking about. It was true, it was happening. The water was rising.

My brain clicked on fast and I started to rouse my younger sister and cousin. "Get up! Now! We gotta move stuff upstairs before the water gets any higher." They had the same reaction as I had earlier, but I pulled them up out of their warm nests and made them move. Somehow, I was able to see what needed to be done and make it happen.

Having moved to this tiny house in Warrensville Heights the prior summer, we didn't have much furniture, but the 4-foot-long TV-Stereo had to go up. We couldn't afford to lose it. Strength took hold and the big bulky box began making its way to the upper level in the hands of us three kids. Next, we tackled the upholstered stuff, placing those pieces on top of wooden kitchen chairs that would probably survive a soak. The creek was still rising, and time was waning, so, with crossed fingers, we had to leave some things as they were.

While we did the heavy lifting, our frantic mother, who could not swim, was packing a Samsonite suitcase with enough clothes for a week's trip to the lake. We lived within walking distance of a shopping center and plenty of places to get provisions, but fear had taken over and she could not be reasoned with.

We set out for the exodus. Through the front door, across our patch of lawn, and down into the street we went. Reaching the canal that was our former street, we forged ahead until the water reached the tops of our skinny white thighs. I couldn't resist being the adventurous one, so I swam through the creek's surplus to the other side while the others walked carrying suitcases and other valuables. Reaching the opposite side, we climbed the small hill to the neighbors' front yard to safety.

Within the hour the rain had stopped, and the water was starting to recede. Dad returned home from his night shift surprised to find us standing on the shore of the road across from our home. He told us that suspecting the creek could overflow its banks, he had snuck out of work earlier to drive by the house to check. All had seemed safe then.

We recounted our adventure to him and were hailed as heroes. His kids had stepped up and taken control. I think this was the first time I had ever heard him say he was proud of us. The one thing we so desperately hoped for and the one thing that we didn't get was his admission that our move to Cleveland had been a mistake and a promise to take us home.

None of us were happy about that, but we needed to stay there in that city and continue to persevere. Our family needed a paycheck and Dad was too old to start over at a new job. We would sell the house because we couldn't live in fear of the creek, but the next house would still be in Ohio.

The saddest part is that we put the house on the market and someone else chose it as their new home. The next summer the creek won again. The three little kids in the yard after the 1969 flood were too young to understand, too small to help, and there was no Daddy. •

Cheryl Powell lives in Winston Salem, North Carolina, where she is a member of the Winston Salem Writers Group. She has been writing stories throughout her adult life and enjoys sharing them with friends and family through letters and emails. She also tells her stories in painting and drawings and has illustrated two children's books.

Bent Not Broken

by Russell Rechenbach

Regretfully, I set the sign near the road overlooking my house on Redhouse. My work was done; the house was ready for sale—new carpets, baseboards, and paint. The day of departure was clear and warm. The neighbor next door was baking fudge. I had loved living there—the charm of the surrounding hills, the lights of the slow-moving train at night, the soft sounds of the creek, the chimes playing in the wind on the big, wrap-around porch with its swing, the patter of rain on the tin roof. As I left the sign to do its magic and to return to my father's farm just a ridge away, I could not help but ponder the tall tree in the distance looming with buzzards.

The next morning, I was awakened by a phone call telling me that Redhouse had flooded. The water had come over the road. I laughed to myself knowing that such a thing was impossible. Then they said the lady next door had climbed into her attic with her cat and had been rescued by a boat.

It was worse than I had expected when I saw it for myself. The waters had receded, leaving behind contaminated mud, debris, and flattened fences. The neighbor on the other side, trying to flee in her car, had to swim out its windows, and public media ridiculed her for driving into a flowing creek. She showed me a video on her phone of the water tearing through my house. My heart broke.

Thirteen years before, I had restored the little farm house in my pitiful effort to save a little patch of Kentucky history. It was built prior to the Civil War along Otter Creek, the old path for Daniel Boone to Fort Boonesborough. The tall cedar trees in the front yard held memories of over a hundred years, some with branches bent from storms but still standing against the adversities of time. Bent, not broken.

The house had been gutted. It had dirt floors and tree branches for studs in its walls. I had it rebuilt. It was not in a flood plain, and all relatives of those who had lived there vouched that it had never been flooded. It had been the heart of the old farm, but slowly its fields gave way to new constructions. It was to be home and a refuge for my daughter and me after a devastating divorce. We thought nobody could ever take it away.

The weeks after the flood were filled with exhausting work: pulling the mud drenched carpets out of the house, cleaning, drying. And no one came to help. Meetings with FEMA only revealed that they could not help me because I had not been living in the house. The water had come from the new development in town, making its way to the Kentucky River through numerous creeks. And because this water came so quickly it pushed tons of rock from the highlands downstream to block the little creeks. The Army Corps of Engineers refused to clear out the creeks; and, they fined farmers who tried to do it themselves.

All my money had gone into Redhouse. I could not have afforded the additional flood insurance, and several authorities had advised me not to get it. I was forced to drop the price on the sale lower and lower with each passing day. And with it my dreams for the future. I too had been beaten down. "Take this," I finally pleaded to God. "Make something good of it."

My agent called to say I had an offer; it was less than a fourth of the original asking price. It came from a family who would live upstairs while working on the downstairs. I went to the closing. They were good people, but life had been unfair to them. They had lived in a storage unit for two years without electricity or water. The mother told their sad story, tears running down her face. Down the face of the real estate agent. Down the face of the lawyer. From the eyes of father and young son. "We prayed and prayed," they wept. "And now, for the first time, we have our own home."

Prayers intersect like streams. A miracle had taken place and I had been a part of it. I took inventory of my life: I was alive and healthy, I had a place to live and I had family. Like those old beaten cedars in the front yard, we all continued to stand, bent, yes, but not broken. •

The Rev. Dr. Russell R. Rechenbach is a native of Frankfort,

Bent Not Broken

Kentucky. He is a graduate of Transylvania University and Lexington Theological Seminary. He has restored the Old Parsonage of Andrew Tribble built 1794. Dr. Rechenbach retired from ministry after 38 years to write historical dramas under the pen name Richard Cavendish.

Broken Dream

by Carole Coates

All Daddy ever wanted was to be a farmer. Knee-high to a mosquito, he helped with farm chores. In grade school, his days began before dawn, milking cows and chopping wood.

After high school, Daddy continued to work the farm with his dad. Two years later, he met Mama. She was heading to Western Carolina Teachers College. He quickly enrolled at North Carolina State. His dreams of farming followed him; he would major in agricultural economics. In one of the many letters that flew between them he wrote, "I aim to own a farm someday."

World War II interrupted Daddy's studies when his ROTC unit was activated. After only a few weeks at Fort Bragg, however, he was honorably discharged—the Army had too many new recruits. Daddy didn't return to school. The military had taken over much of the campus. Besides, his patriotism demanded he find another way to help the war effort. First, he worked in the Newport News shipyard, then at Union Carbide in New Jersey.

That was too far from Mama. When Daddy was offered a transfer to the new "Secret City" of Oak Ridge, Tennessee, he leapt at the opportunity.

Daddy and Mama married. The war ended. I was born. A year later, Daddy's farm-owning dream came true. With help from Mama's parents, he and Mama purchased a mountain farm on the banks of the Tuckaseegee River just a few miles from where she grew up.

Disaster struck almost immediately. Daddy kept a hundred chicks in a brooder box on the back porch. One frigid morning, he found all of them frozen. He could not afford more.

Daddy tried growing sweet potatoes at river's edge. It worked back home. (Did I mention that Daddy grew up in eastern North Carolina?) The old man who came with the place told him it was no good. But Daddy, with the ignorant arrogance of youth, paid him no heed. After all, he knew farming. He'd studied the latest techniques.

The old man was right, of course. The soil, the rainfall, the temperature—they all were different here. The crop failed. The old-timer's thoughts must have run along the lines of Olive Tilford Dargan's neighbor in *From My Highest Hill* when he said about a certain "book-farmer" from Raleigh, "Maybe he knowed all about flat-land farmin' but the world couldn't hold what he didn't know about raisin' corn in this 'jump-up' country."

Bryan, Daddy's youngest brother, came to help out for a couple weeks after his freshman year at Mars Hill College. When Granddaddy came to pick him up, Bryan took another look around, recalled how desperately poor our little family was, knew how urgently Daddy needed help, and said, "Daddy, I can't leave." In exchange, Daddy offered to pay Bryan's bus fare back to school come fall.

Daddy grew rye and wheat. The previous owner had left an old combine behind. None of the nearby farmers had such a machine. With a lot of elbow grease and some baling wire (a farmer's best friend), Daddy and Bryan got the combine in working order. Bryan hired out to cut the neighbors' fields. But there was no demand for grain that year. All the farmers could offer in payment was the one thing Daddy didn't need—more grain. He didn't have two nickels for Bryan's return trip.

It took only a year for Daddy to figure out his farming dream had died, and ever after, it pained him to talk about that year. But without another source of income, we'd soon be homeless. Daddy found a non-farm job that led to another and another until he retired years later as vice-president of the insurance subsidiaries of what had become, through a series of mergers, Bank of America.

Daddy never lost his love of the land, though. Wherever my parents lived, he grew a garden. He gave away more food than he and Mama kept for themselves. He couldn't help himself. Only one home could not accommodate a garden. That was when Daddy experienced a near-fatal heart attack. The prognosis gave him only a couple more years. Daddy and Mama moved again, this time to a place with an extra lot. Daddy was back to gardening, giving it up only shortly before his death from congestive heart failure thirteen years later.

I believe Daddy was happiest when he had dirt under his fingernails. I guess you can take the farmer off the farm, but you can't take the farm out of the farmer. •

Carole Coates lives in a self-built home in Watauga County, North Carolina. She has published *Boyhood Daze and Other Stories: Growing Up Happy During the Great Depression* and *Living on the Diagonal: Mountain Musings*. You can find her blog at https://livingonthediagonal.com. She also blogs for Mother Earth News Magazine. Coates is currently working on a book about her mother's childhood.

Adieu Encore

by Sallie Showalter

I never seemed to be able to keep a job. Oh, sure, I could get a good job and, toward the end of my ill-fated career, even an interesting job. A job I loved. And I would go at it with gusto, pouring every fiber of my being into finding creative solutions to recalcitrant problems, coaxing colleagues into trying new ways of tackling the same old issues, learning new tools and adopting new technology, and occasionally even getting recognized for my efforts.

But after two or three years, I would find myself in the same situation: burned out, frustrated, exhausted, tired of battling the same demons. It just didn't seem worth devoting my limited days on this earth to something that was making me so miserable.

So I would quit. And I would find another job. I always did. I was somehow able to convince employers that I had skills that would help make them successful. And that was true. I would work myself to the brink of death to meet deadlines. I would compulsively check my work and the work of my colleagues to make sure it didn't have mistakes that would put the company at risk. I would be the one with the courage to lead my team through impossible predicaments.

I was a good employee. The companies and organizations I worked for certainly got their money's worth. But I secretly knew I wouldn't last long, even if I were absolutely, 100 percent committed to making this new situation the one I would stay in forever.

Then, one day, I left a job with good prospects for other employment. But something happened. This time I couldn't nail that other job. My little scheme had run its course. They were on to me.

So I became a writer. This job doesn't pay anything. In fact, it's become quite expensive. I can only continue because of the largess of my absurdly patient husband. He must love me. Or be amused by me. Otherwise he would have found a reliable, hard-working, income-earning wife a long time ago. He has the charm to do that, any time he wants. But, for some reason, he's stuck by me.

Which brings me to how I learned why I am the way I am. I became a writer, in part, because two stories dropped in my lap—two family stories that just had to be told. This is interesting in itself, because I never had much interest in family history and I had never wanted to be a writer.

One of these stories involves my maternal grandfather. He was born in Paris, Kentucky, into a prominent family with ties back to the American Revolution. When he was in his late 20s, after returning from World War I, he married an educated woman with a promising teaching career from a nearby town. Within a year, they had a daughter, my mother.

And then he disappeared.

Try as I might, I could not find anyone in my family who knew where he went or what happened to him. They either did not know, did not want to share what they did know, or truly did not care what fate had befallen him. All signs indicated he had simply absconded, leaving behind a wife who had given up her career to marry him and a newborn daughter.

Fast-forward to the Internet Age, and a conversation with my neighbor—an accomplished investigative reporter—led to unraveling my grandfather's tale. The first clues appear five years after his disappearance, when he marries another woman in Cincinnati. He attests on the marriage application that he has "never been married before and has no wife living." Yet, he shares his birthplace and identifies his parents by name.

He does this three more times. Every two or three years, in fact, he leaves what appears to be a good job as a chef at a sizable hotel or other large establishment and moves on. When he arrives in a new city, he finds a new wife. No records indicate he ever took care of any legal niceties relating to the previous marriage. For whatever reason, he simply became unhappy with the situation and he left.

It is perverse, I admit, but I feel so much better knowing that my restlessness is hereditary. I have failed, over and over. But, ultimately, I have found a job I love. I'm discovering clues about who I am. I'm connecting with people I never would have met and learning more every day about why we are who we are.

And my husband, a native of Paris, Kentucky, is still here, cheering me on.

At least he was the last I checked . . . •

Sallie Showalter lives in Georgetown, Kentucky, with her patient husband and demanding dog. She is currently a student in the Author Academy at the Carnegie Center for Literacy & Learning in Lexington, Kentucky., and recently published *The Last Resort: Journal of a Salt River Camp 1942-43*. Next up: a novel about her grandfather's life. You can follow her blog at www.murkypress.com/blog.

Mirror, Mirror ...

by Robin Hurdle

How did a girl from a small community in North Carolina find herself in the world of celebrities and millionaires? I wasn't looking for fame and fortune; I just wanted to be a model and the closest I could get to that dream was to work for a sports marketing group.

When I was young I would look at pictures of beautiful women in magazines and I wanted to be like them. My perception of beauty was based on hearing my father describe a beautiful woman. I learned that beautiful women had value; fat women were lazy. He joked about "trading in" an older woman for a younger one without wrinkles or gray hair. My father would say, "It's about time to trade in this 40 for two 20s." Although it was a joke, at my impressionable age, it was hard to know what was a joke and what was reality.

I struggled in school with a listening disability and low self-esteem, so my looks were the only thing going for me. The pressure to fit into that mold defined who I was for the next 30 years. I would look in the mirror and pick apart all my flaws. I felt like I wasn't perfect in my eyes, much less anyone else's.

To me, if a person were smart, they would always be smart; they wouldn't suddenly wake up stupid one morning. But if you were known for your good looks, you only had a small window of time to take advantage of it. Even when I was at the peak of my dream job, I still couldn't enjoy it. I felt like I was always being judged.

My career was based on my looks and friendly personality, but sometimes men would assume they could take advantage of the situation or use their influence to manipulate me. Some people question the "#Me Too" movement that is happening now, but I experienced what has happened to so many women.

In the 80s, it seemed that many men (and maybe women, but I can't say for sure) in careers that required them to travel frequently felt it was innocent fun to see how far they could go with someone. And if they went all the way, that was okay - what happened on the road stayed on the road. It was a game to them, but to me, my job was on the line. Worse yet was the way they acted so innocent in public - devoted husband and family man. I looked at them with their wives and wondered if they knew about their husband's little games.

While I was on the road, the company I worked for would have its representatives put together gift packages for events. Since we were traveling to different states, we didn't have the use of offices or conference rooms, so we worked in one of our hotel rooms. One time a team member destroyed my room trying to force himself on me. Another time someone I trusted and respected dropped his pants and asked me "Do you like this?" While at a party in New York, a well-known celebrity forced me into a bathroom and locked the door, even though his wife was in the next room.

When I told my supervisors about the incident in the hotel room, I was told that perhaps I "misunderstood" his advancements. What about the hotel damages and my torn dress, I asked? The company would pay for both, but they advised me to drop the matter. I got the message: I could be easily replaced, but he was protected because of his value to the company.

Even though these memories still haunt me, I also remember the good times. Where else could a small-town girl have the opportunity to travel all over the United States in first class? I loved the travel and meeting people from all walks of life. And the years I traveled helped me to grow stronger and more confident.

You would think now that I am in my 50s, I would be able to accept and embrace aging with grace, but the truth is, I struggle with it every day. I look into the mirror and wish I could see the young woman I once was staring back at me. I am haunted by the words of men from years ago as they joked about women they knew: She let herself go. She is so fat. She must be lazy. What happened to that sparkle in her eyes?

Mirror, Mirror ...

I am living through this next chapter in my life. One day I will look beyond the mirror and see the true reflection. The small-town girl and I will love me for me. •

Robin H. Hurdle lives in Lexington, North Carolina, where she and her husband have a small business. They have two adult sons and three dogs. Robin's story, "Postcards from the Heart," appeared in the Winston-Salem Chronicle in 2015 and in a publication for Forsyth Technical Community College. She enjoys traveling, photography, and painting.

Banking on Yoga

by Deborah Rankin

I opened my eyes a slit to sneak a look at the women around me. They sat on thin mats, eyes closed, in a room where candle light flickered over their earnest faces and silken cloths with scenes of forest, sunset, and wave-foamed sea fluttered on the walls behind them. Scents of sandalwood and rosemary filled the room. The plaintive wail of an ancient stringed instrument encircled the space, reverberating between the high tin ceiling and polished wood floor.

Our leader read a closing poem. We clasped our hands in prayer, chanted, bowed heads, and murmured thanks. I forced myself into a routine doxology: *Thank you for my safe home … health … eyes to see and ears to hear … the delicious quiche waiting in the oven at home, made from local eggs, Swiss chard and basil from my garden … I wonder which wine will pair best with it?*

I forced my mind from my growling stomach, and lingered, savoring bliss, until I laughed out loud at the absurdity of the situation. Fifteen women sat on yoga mats in the building where my grandmother used to bank!

She was born in an isolated Kentucky valley 120 years ago and died 28 years before this day of yoga hilarity. She drove horse-drawn carriages and Ford Model-As, and flew in an airplane once, at age 84, to visit me in Houston. Though she stopped school after sixth grade, she pushed her offspring to get education. Her eldest child, daughter Connie, was the first person from the valley to graduate high school. Second-born Geneva was the first to attend college. Her grandchildren include a physician, dentist, veterinarian, university professor, school teachers, business leaders, and entrepreneurs. I wondered what she would find most surprising about my life: the life-altering advances in transportation and technology, or the sight of sane women paying good money to lie on the former bank floor with strangers, breathing in and out together, propping their legs up the walls?

My 5-foot-4-inch grandmother, whom I called "Memie," was a powerhouse of influence. She carried buckets of water into the house from the cistern so she and her family could eat, drink, and wash. She poured boiling water into a hand-cranked wringer to clean the family's clothes, then lugged sodden garments outside to hang them by clothes pins on a wire. During the Depression, she fed and housed "boarders"—railroad men building a new tunnel for the track between Cincinnati and Lexington—strangers who slept upstairs in the unfurnished attic in exchange for precious cash she used to buy shoes, tools, and medicine.

What if I brought that tough and determined little woman into my world? Told her she had enough money to buy machines for her manual work, with enough left over for a large, comfortable car she could drive to the bank to meet friends, listen to beautiful music, and relax while a kind person rubbed sweet-smelling oil on her temples? That woman would recognize a good thing when she saw it. She'd waste no time slipping into Lycra and getting on the mat.

I came to yoga that night feeling sorry for myself. In the last two years, I had watched my beloved father lose a horrible struggle with cancer, received an unexpected pink slip from my high-paying corporate job, suffered serious health problems, and sold my large home with a pool and a view to move into a friend's garage to save money. Then I moved back home to Kentucky and took a job that paid half my previous salary.

When I brought Memie into the studio of my imagination, I saw my world through her eyes. Despite a smaller job and tighter budget and regardless of my aching heart and thwarted dreams, I could still afford yoga, movies, a home with running water, and a washing machine. I was rich. My hands did not have to launder a strange man's sheets, nor scrape the plates from which he ate breakfast.

After I laughed at our banking yoga studio, everything changed. What I'd called "turkeys"—unwanted life changes—taught me gratitude for blessings I had overlooked. I remembered again what I learned from my father after his painful and slow death. When I cleaned out his desk the day after his funeral, I found these words written on a note pad in his strong, clear script:

> *Life is not about waiting for the storms to pass.*
> *It's about learning to dance in the rain.*

Banking on Yoga

Rest in peace, beloved father. I am learning that dance. •

Deborah Rankin lives in Scott County, Kentucky, where her family has farmed for over 200 years. After writing four highly technical medical research papers, she now works on a memoir, a DC-based suspense novel, and a YA/new adult Appalachian family drama. Everything she is today she owes to her parents' and grandparents' examples and encouragements to keep *bearing up*.

The Brick

by Howard Pearre

I was eleven, and for weeks the excitement consumed me—my first scout camp and the swimming merit badge course. Being in the water was what I lived for.

What I had not counted on was a bad case of homesickness. Despite an array of crafts, hikes, and other daytime activities, the nights included plenty of empty time available for childlike worry.

I imagined terrible events—car crashes, fires. I imagined I would never see my parents again. While I was determined to complete the week, I craved to make "the call" to plead with my father to drive the twenty miles from Charlotte, to bring me home and save me from my misery. Late one night, one of the counselors resorted to strumming a guitar and singing M-I-C K-E-Y M-O-U-S-E to help me overcome my anxiety.

Mornings were completely different. I would discover I'd actually gotten some sleep, and the first activity was the swimming badge course.

Each day the boys—I was the youngest, barely old enough even to attend the camp, as well as the skinniest and weakest—gathered at the lake's edge.

In a week, for two hours each morning, we would learn and then demonstrate swimming proficiency. We'd tackle the four basic strokes: crawl, side, back, and breast. We'd venture beyond the safety rope for a distance swim. We'd demonstrate the ability to float for several minutes. I'd fill my chest with air and fling my arms as far out as possible. But then, due to my skin-and-bones physique, my legs and feet would quickly sink and curl beneath my body, my nose barely protruding the surface.

The merit badge handbook described the final exercise this way: In water over your head, but not to exceed 10 feet, perform a surface dive and bring an object up from the bottom.

Simple if you're in a clear pool. Not so simple if you're in a lake where light dies a foot from the surface.

The instructor stood on the floating dock.

"In my hand I have a brick. Your task is to retrieve it. You will perform a surface dive, locate the brick, and bring it to me."

Several other boys attempted the task, each one successfully producing the brick on his first attempt. I was glad for them but concerned for me. I had been to the bottom of that lake before.

My turn came. I jumped in and treaded water. The instructor tossed the brick several yards away from my position. Eyeing the point where the brick had splashed, I positioned my body into a horizontal attitude and dove.

Down I swam, headfirst. Three feet below the surface there was nothing but darkness. I continued pushing my body downward. I came to the bottom of the lake. I could see nothing and felt only soft loose mud and yuck. I felt all around with both hands. I searched and searched and breathed out the spent air as slowly as possible. The oxygen was quickly dissipating from my lungs. When the air was gone, I gave up, shot to the surface and gasped.

The instructor did not smile. He simply made a downward motion with an index finger.

I inhaled to absolute full-lung capacity and went down, down again near the same spot. This time I swam in a pattern near the area I thought would yield the brick. And again, after all usable air was expelled, and my lungs were screaming, I rushed to the surface.

Filling my lungs with air, I headed for the bottom for my third try. I swam in a tight circular pattern near where I thought the brick would be. Around and around, desperately digging into the bottom with my fingers, I felt every square inch. No brick. I stayed even longer this time. Had my search buried the brick? With my body aching from the wild exercise and with no discernable oxygen left in my lungs, I gave up, defeated.

As I turned for the surface my toe grazed something solid. Instantly, I knew it was the brick, and I knew I had to go back, or I would never find it again. I turned downward and reached my hand to where my toe had been a moment before.

I felt and felt in the watery mud. My body cried for oxygen, but there was none left in my lungs. At the last possible second, my hand found the brick. I worked it loose and dashed to the surface, breaking the water, gasping, gulping air, holding the brick high.

That swimming merit badge was the first one to go on my sash. And I had made it through the week without making that call. •

Howard Pearre retired in 2015 after a career as a counselor and manager with NC Vocational Rehabilitation and the Veterans Administration. He lives in Winston-Salem, North Carolina, where he is a member of Winston-Salem Writers. His short fiction pieces have appeared in Second Spring and Silver Arts publications. He has six grandchildren, avoids Saturday crossword puzzles, and makes fig wine.

What Survives the Family Road Trips
by Grace Ellis

It was the 1950s and early 1960s, before the interstate highway system, before seat belt rules, before hand-held entertainment devices. Our family vacations involved traveling from our home in Alabama—and later in Kentucky—to visit relatives or beaches or conference centers. Although we fondly remember kissing our cousins hello and goodbye, the tugboats in the canal at Gulf Shores, and the armadillo who scratched his back beneath the floorboards in our house at MoRanch, our clearest memories are of the journeys themselves.

Our expedition would begin when we assembled our bags and the camping equipment—tents, air mattresses and sleeping bags, a bicycle pump, a cooler, a picnic basket, a camp cookware set, and a Coleman camp stove—for my father to arrange in the "way back" section of our station wagon. Then our mother, our father, and the four of us piled in and took off. Of course, we children picked fights with each other, but our parents did a good job of keeping us engaged in various activities as we drove down the old winding highways.

We counted the "See Rock City" signs on barn roofs and read

aloud the Burma Shave signs. We tried to break our previous records for the number of different state license tags spotted. We played the alphabet game, trying to find the letters of the alphabet in order on the billboards we passed (welcoming the Quality Oil or Texaco signs). Later, when we'd had more advanced math courses, we tried to form equations from the numbers on license plates. We divided into two teams (right side and left side) to play "cow poker" with its complex rules. Points were gained by counting cows, horses, sheep, goats, or chickens visible on your team's side of the road. Extra points (rarely earned) came for ducks on a pond or a cat in a window. A junkyard on a team's side would cut its points in half and a graveyard would wipe them out entirely—but only if spotted by the other team. None of us ever glimpsed the red-headed girl on a white mule that would have signaled a game-ending victory.

My brother James would be given one hour each day to lead us in singing with his ukulele. Then there would be the brief rest stops at filling stations, where we would get the car filled with gas and visit the restrooms, and our parents would buy a pack of chewing gum and give each of us one stick. Around noon, we all had to watch for the signs identifying roadside picnic tables, where we could stop, unpack the picnic basket, and eat lunch.

As the day wore on, my father would give the wheel to my mother and demand silence as he composed the narrative for the next chapter in his chronicle of the adventures of the pirate captain Tidmore C. Jones and his crew. The stories incorporated events and sights from the day's journey. One story had the president of Dahlonega State Teachers' College, which we had recently passed, kidnapping Tidmore C. Jones's gum-chewing secretary, Yolanda Yvonne Smackjaws, by sticking her to his office chair with a wad of her chewing gum. Once, my mother became so entranced by the stories that she drove off the route completely, taking what my father later assured her had been a shortcut to our destination.

In the late afternoon, within an hour or so of the state park where we planned to spend the night, we would squirm and whine in the car as my mother stopped at a grocery store to get the supplies for our next three meals. My father then drove to the park and found a campsite. My mother would cook supper on the Coleman stove while the rest of us pitched the two pup tents and the larger umbrella tent and pumped up our air mattresses for the night. Frequently, the big tent collapsed on my father when he moved the center pole.

We fell asleep to the sound of frogs and crickets, and in the morning, we woke when my father unscrewed the caps to deflate our air mattresses. We got up, visited the restrooms, got dressed, helped to take down the tents, and after breakfast at the picnic table, re-packed the car and took off again.

What by now must be obvious to anyone reading this account is something that we four children never realized until we were grown: Our parents could only afford vacations on the cheap. Really, really on the cheap. But here's the thing: Not only did we never feel deprived; these hardscrabble, summer road trips provided us with what are now, hands down, the most precious memories of our childhood. •

Family Road Trips

Grace Ellis lives in Clemmons, North Carolina. She is a member of Winston-Salem Writers, the Greensboro Playwrights Forum, and the Dramatists Guild. Grace has written more than two dozen plays, and watched them performed in school auditoriums, churches, theaters, and orchards. She also writes essays and poems and occasionally blogs at https://gracewinnellis.com.

A Mother's Ingenuity
by Antoinette Sirois

C all it a plan, a scheme, a trick. My mother was artfully cunning when it came to saving her family.

My parents were part of the large immigration to America that took place early in the 20th Century. As were so many others who came, they were seeking a better life. They chose, like many other Sicilian/Italian immigrants, to go to Syracuse, New York.

My father's trade was carpentry; he had skills. Life was good in the early years of their marriage. Pa had steady work. He built a house for the rapidly growing family of five children. My mother made it a home. Several relatives also came to America and joined them to live in Syracuse. They were all becoming established in the church, in the community and they were making new friends.

The Great Depression changed it all. Pa could no longer find work. They could not make the mortgage payments, so they lost their much-loved family home.

When my father heard there was work to be found in Gloversville, a smaller city about 100 miles north and east of Syracuse, my parents had no choice but to move, leaving behind their relatives, their community, and their new friends.

Pa went first. He took a bus to Gloversville to find a place for the family to live. When he returned, he told my mother the only affordable rental housing was in a 24-unit apartment housing project named The Century Block. Ma said, "*E buono.*" Pa shook his head, saying, "No, not good. There is one big problem. Rules are: only two children per family permitted in each unit."

Most of us heard my father's words as an insurmountable problem, short of eliminating three children. But, my mother was not so quick to be discouraged. It didn't take her long to come up with a plan.

She proposed the family move into the apartment with the two youngest children, leaving the older three children temporarily behind to stay with relatives. After a month or two, my father was to make regular bus trips back to Syracuse and, one at a time, bring each of the children back to rejoin the family. Ma believed that when the manager of the housing complex saw what a fine, law-abiding, clean, and God-loving family we were, the two-children-per-family rule would be ignored. My father went along, saying, "We have nothing to lose." And, soon enough, with the cooperation of relatives, we put Ma's plan in motion.

Ma decided that two months after the initial move was long enough to establish the family's good reputation. She put phase two of her plan into action. Pa began his monthly trips back to Syracuse, returning with one more child. Soon all five children were living in the apartment. And, Ma's plan worked as she had predicated; the landlord accepted each addition to our family without comment.

Because the manager had disregarded the regulation for our family, it was not long before other families had more than two children in their apartments, too. Those families thanked my parents many times for what they did to get that rule lifted.

And it was a good thing they had done so. Six years after the move to Gloversville, my parents added another child. Not quite two years after that, Ma gave birth to her seventh child, my youngest sibling. We were then a family of nine living in the apartment designed for a family of no more than four. And we were close—yes, very close—in every sense of the word.

Our family lived in the housing project for 12 years. But when an opportunity arose to move out of that cramped apartment and into a home of our own, once again, my resourceful and amazing mother put her mind to work and made a difference for her family. •

Copyright 2018, Antoinette Sirois

Antoinette Vecchio Sirois lives in Concord, North Carolina. After

A Mother's Ingenuity

September 11, 2001, she wrote her first and only poem; it was published. After six decades, she left her life-long state of New York to retire in North Carolina, where she began writing her life stories for her children and grandchildren.

Show-and-Tell Goddess
by Diane Pascoe

I can tell when it's autumn in Daniel Boone country because my Love God abandons washing the car with his fluffy wool mitt and instead watches hunting and fishing shows beamed into our home from the wild yonder.

As I watch the hunting shows, my thoughts drift back to my childhood. I can clearly remember the deer my father brought home, and the packages of venison wrapped in brown paper which then filled the freezer. It was a mystery meat that Dad tried to pass off as grade A Angus beef. We never seemed to run out of those Bambi bundles, and I was just as happy when our power went out and the thawed, ruined meat had to be destroyed. It isn't the venison, but the dead deer's leg, that I recall nostalgically—the one that was removed just above the knee and then nicely cleaned up. I didn't know what I would ever do with that thing, but when my turn for show-and-tell arrived, I suddenly knew.

Show-and-tell was my favorite activity at school because I had the spotlight to talk about anything I wanted, and nobody would pull me off the stage. Filled with anticipation the night before this event, I usually wandered around the house looking for that special item that would fill my classmates with awe and envy. No picture books or tacky tourist ashtrays of Niagara Falls for this girl. I was going for the big bang, the loud applause, the cheers of lesser gods. So, when I found the deer's leg in the toy box, I knew I had found my ticket to fame.

I didn't connect the leg to a deceased animal with antlers. It was just a dead deer's leg—fur, hoof, ligaments, and all—which we kept in the toy box amid the baseballs, skipping ropes, and roller skates. The leg had a life of its own, and I mean that literally, because when you tugged the ligament just above the knee, the hoof moved. Back and forth, back and forth—
I tugged that ligament until the hoof looked like it was waving, much like a queen waving at her subjects. Once Buzzy Munroe saw that magnificent moving leg, I knew he'd choose me to be his girlfriend instead of beautiful Jennifer Eadie with her movie-star name.

In my hoof-waving dreams, I became a show-and-tell goddess, better than even Rosalyn with the wavy blond Marilyn Monroe hair, who could only muster up her leaf collection that she had ironed with wax paper and put in her Beehive Corn Syrup scrapbook. Deer's leg versus scrapbook, Diane versus Rosalyn. I would win hoofs down.

When my big moment finally came, I was not disappointed. The glory unfolded exactly as I had imagined. I pulled the leg out of the flowered pillowcase for all to gawk at. Oohs and aahs filled the room. I ignored the grimace on Rosalyn's face— she knew she'd met her match. The teacher screeched with delight, or maybe horror, and all the boys, including Buzzy, moved in for a closer inspection. This was the recognition I cherished.

As I retired to my seat, dead deer's leg grasped in my hand, I knew I had moved to the show-and-tell Hall of Fame. You could only play the dead deer's leg card once at school, but that was OK—it wasn't that easy lugging around a deer's leg anyway. The leg would retire to the toy box, perhaps for another sister to drag out to secure her popularity.

Though I don't think I will ever get used to the sight of a fallen deer, I am thankful that one such creature gave up its life and leg for show-and-tell history and the fond memories of this one-time child star. •

Diane and husband Eric, (aka "Honey" or "Love God"), retired to Leland, North Carolina in 2016 after many years in Raleigh. Along with winning several North Carolina writing contests, Diane's humor essays are published monthly in Wilmington-area publications.

The Call
by Linda Freudenberger

The light on the console blinked as the phone rang gently in the parish office; I answered it quickly. I was the only one there following choir practice. The voice at the other end came from a woman full of anguish. She asked to speak to the parish priest. I told her at the moment we had an interim priest but that she had stepped out of the office.

"Can I help?" I inquired. She explained that her mother was receiving hospice care and had requested visits from the Episcopal church.

"I am a lay minister," I offered. "I would be glad to come administer the sacraments of Holy Communion and the laying-on of hands for healing, if you would like." We made arrangements for me to visit her mother Marie on Thursday.

When I arrived at the modest, split-foyer home, I was greeted warmly by the woman who had called. Her name was Linda. I also met her teenaged daughter Holly and her husband, Jim. She led me down the hall to the bedroom where Marie lay on a twin-sized bed, bundled in quilts. A Yankee Candle burned,

The Call

165

releasing the flowery scent of gardenias. Later I would learn this was Marie's favorite flower. Marie smiled at me as I arrived, and she portrayed a genuine welcome in her eyes and voice.

I learned Marie's story as I came once a week to provide communion for her and her family. She had terminal liver cancer; there was no treatment. Marie was being cared for by her daughter, son-in-law, and granddaughter. She had three other grown children who lived far away in three different states. Marie was always glad to see me and had a certain spark, I thought, in her kind eyes.

I found this whole scene quite healing to me. About a year earlier, I had lost my mother while caring for her in my home with help from hospice. But my mother totally withdrew from us and turned her back to me and my husband; she would sleep a lot. That situation was very painful for me. Being with Marie was healing for me; to see someone who was dying but who was still reaching out was a comfort. It was a blessing.

One week, I called to tell Linda that I could not make it the next Thursday but would send someone else in my place. On Wednesday morning, she called to say Marie was declining quickly and she was not sure if Marie would survive until Thursday. I rushed over Wednesday to give them communion and to offer prayers. Linda had gathered favorite family photos of her mom and put them in an album which she shared with me that morning along with many happy memories.

Linda called the next day to say Marie had passed two hours

after I left. That day of her passing was the first anniversary of my own mother's passing! Linda asked if I would speak at Marie's memorial service; I readily accepted the invitation.

I believe God places us in each others' paths for a reason. Linda told me I was a great comfort to her since she could ask me questions about dealing with her mom's pain and her own spiritual needs. She also shared that the hospice journey was very difficult for her. Linda was an occupational therapist. Her job was to rehabilitate people and to get them back to their lives, not to prepare them for death. I shared with Linda that Marie had been, and continued to be, an angel for me because I had been aching from the way my mom turned away from me during her last days.

Marie's gentle passing was a journey for all of us, a union, a convergence, and a crossing of the paths of several pilgrims. And, that phone call was no coincidence. That blinking light was a gentle wink from a loving God. •

Linda Freudenberger lives in Lexington, Kentucky, where she studies non-fiction and memoir writing at the Carnegie Center for Literacy and Learning. A recently retired occupational therapist, she serves as a volunteer tutor at the Center's student outreach program. She also enjoys writing to share family memories.

BEARING UP

168

A Circle of Warmth

by Mary Gregory

I have a visual image of a group of friends. We hold hands in a circle. I call it my circle of warmth.

One of the strongest members in her style and soul is Jackie. This is a time I need to pull Jackie into the center of the circle to be surrounded with its love and care.

Jackie is also a colleague. She and I have taught first and second grade together for fifteen years at an independent school in Charlotte, North Carolina. We share an unspoken belief in the goodness of children, in the power of optimism, and we practice dignity and self-respect around our children and fellow teachers. We encourage our students to demonstrate civility in speaking and in manners toward adults, as we try to model considerate and courteous behavior. We treat each other and the other friend-teachers with whom we work so closely this way.

That is one of our work-related common bonds.

My care for Jackie goes beyond this. She is a shining face in my circle of warmth outside of work. I call her when I need advice. She is one of the few people with whom I share vulnerabilities. I trust her love and her judgment. She is practical where I am vague; directed where I am meandering.

But now, I am scared, and for this reason.

She came to me on the playground last Friday. Surrounding us were shrieking children, free and happy to be let loose to run and play on an early autumn day. Amidst their shrieks and squeals and zigzag runs, their kickball dodgings and jungle-gym glee, she reached for my hand. Holding it, she said, "There are rumors flying and I wanted you to know. I won't be here next Thursday." In my quick-reaction-no-reflection first-grade-teacher mode, I bluntly uttered, "Why? What's up?"

She said four words which chilled my bones. The chill returns again, as I write.

"I have breast cancer."

The juxtaposition of this reality, in the midst of the children's playground world, was surreal.

As with such news, explanation and information were

exchanged. However, underneath the data and detail, we came to this, together, there on the playground: Our hope comes first; optimism reigns. You can think only the best in such a situation. There is no other choice from which to proceed. Together we almost forcefully, adamantly, pushed fear away, and we embraced our common walk of positive outcome and grace under pressure.

Yet, I am afraid. She is afraid. The lurking reality of how easily the world we know becomes unhinged lies at our feet.

Until the surgery is performed, each day when I think of Jackie, she stands in the center of the circle. All the warmth of love from others shines on her. She basks in our glow. She accepts our affirmations. And we will be there in all seasons, to help her heal, so she in turn, can return to the outer edges, and become one with us again.

The above piece was written about nine years ago. Jackie's surgery was successful and she has been cancer-free since then. Just last week, we met for our usual once-a-month coffee talks at Panera Bread. Now, both retired from teaching, we continue our friendship. She had more news: "They found a new spot. I go in for a biopsy next week."

I went back to this piece I had written. In it, I find what I need once again to move forward with her on this new leg of our journey. No longer are we in the circle of warmth from our school, but it remains in our hearts and minds. We learned early on how to garner the love of people around us to carry us forward. It is from this strength that we move ahead.

We do not know where our journey leads. But whatever happens it will be okay because we will proceed with dignity and optimism and in the circle of warmth from our playground days. That knowledge, in itself, will help us handle the rest. •

Mary Dashiell Gregory lives in Charlotte, North Carolina, where she is a member of the Charlotte Writers Club. Her interest in writing grew with teaching first-graders the joy in finding creative expression through words on paper. A few pieces have appeared in regional and national magazines, and in the anthology *Imagining Heaven*.

Passing Memories
by Barbara Chandler

I've put the plastic up over the windows, just like I helped my Mamaw do when I was little. They didn't have plastic to put up when my mom was little. She and her sisters would glue newspaper over the cracks in the wall to help keep in the heat from the back-to-back fire place. I've used plaster on most of the cracks, but I still have some newspaper stuffed around window frames where I ran out of that terrible, sticky spray foam. It does stop drafts, newspaper does, and it makes me smile.

I touch the window frames my Papaw and Paw Hensley fitted. They are made of old hardwood, and those that have survived need some paint. It's been a while. Maybe in the spring there will be time, money and energy for it. Mamaw wouldn't like the chips in the paint showing wood through 65 years of layers.

We used to paint about every two years, even the floors, and cover them with squares of vinyl rugs that left about six inches of the painted floors showing in every room. Those edges would catch the dirt from the yard and the coal dust from the fireplaces when we swept. We would have to scrub the coal dust out of the textures every month. They would look so new for about a week, then the coal dust was back. Between that and the sulfur in the well water, those rugs didn't stand a chance. The smell of the coal dust and sulfur in the mop water is still strong in my memory. More than bleach or soap, it's the smell that means "cleaning" to me.

Sulfur water is troublesome when you are washing hair or clothes; it messes with the colors and the textures, but I loved the taste of it. We would draw it up with a long bucket on a pulley right outside the kitchen. We would swing the metal well bucket over to the huge lard buckets. They had been used to hold the water so often their insides were orange. By the time I was 5 or 6, I would beg to draw the water so I could get the first drink, cold from the ground. When we moved and had spring water from the mountain on the Harlan road, I didn't like it. I thought it tasted "slick", not rough like the water I was used to.

Brushing the curtains back in place, I guess I am thirsty with all this thought of water. The curtains are old, about 15 years old, but I like them, soft white cotton with dragonflies embroidered. Though I have a few new sheers in the living room, these are in the boys' room. Mom tells me about feed-sack curtains she would help her mother make. The feed for the cows, horses, and pigs would come in bags of colored, patterned cotton. They would make curtains, pillowcases and even clothes for the kids. Mamaw would wash them over and over till they were soft and use brown paper to make patterns. I remember some of the pillowcases, textured cottons with yellow and green flowers or blue birds.

Looking out the window I appreciate that I have a yard. When the house was built, it was on the edge of a hill. Every year after it was built, on breaks in the farming, Papaw and his six kids built the 10 feet of front yard. They hauled boulders and stones and dirt, and over years built a wall 10 feet high and 70 feet long to hold up the yard. I still wonder at it, touching a stone and wondering if it was one my mother rolled, skinny little black-haired thing that she was. Did one of my uncles or my aunts put it there? I know my Papaw touched them all.

All the things about me, they are not kept just because the money needs to go to gas for the car, or electric bills, but because of the hands that touched them. The chair my grandmother bought in the 90s, that she sat in so many times when I visited from college, I can't bear to be rid of it. The table and hutch my Aunt Leoda bought with her American-Greetings-job money are old and scarred, because of my boys mostly. She was so proud to bring them home for her mother. She polished them over and over, filling the house with the scent of Lemon Pledge®. Not just things, these are memories. I am touching where those I loved touched, and trying to pass those stories to my sons, who never had the chance to know them. •

Copyright 2018, Barbara Chandler

Barbara Chandler reared two boys around Fourmile, on the Boone Trace along the Cumberland River in Bell County, Kentucky, where her family has lived for over 100 years. Grandmother Dixie Bell Hensley Sizemore was born there in 1917. Her father, Richard

Hensley, was postmaster and barber for the area. He and Dixie's husband, Johnny, were coal miners and farmers, too.

The Truth at 13

by Randell Jones

I would go back to a lot of ages, but 13 would not be one of them.

I taught first-graders in Sunday School for 15 years. I was older than their parents. I took pictures of the children wearing names tags and posted the pictures on the bulletin board. It helped me learn their names and it gave them a sense of belonging to the group.

After six years, I realized that first group then comprised the current Confirmation Class. So, I took their pictures again in the spring of their seventh-grade year; and, at the Confirmation banquet, I gave them each the two pictures side-by-side in a little booklet, "A Book of Advice You Didn't Ask For, But Got Anyway, Lucky You."

I created a ceremony so all the students could sign each other's books by walking around a table and signing their names every seven seconds as their parents serenaded them in unison with new words I had written to "Tell Me Why." One verse began,

"Tell me why your room's a mess," so you get the idea.

Before the kids got up to encircle the tables, I had to give them some instructions on how we would work this "magic"; and, before I gave them those instructions, I said, I wanted to tell them a story from my own experience at 13 about listening to instructions . . . and not.

When I was your age, I began, we took a few physical education classes to develop our social skills by square dancing. The boys sat on one side of the gym, the girls on the other. The coach would blow his whistle and the boys would race across the gym to pick a partner. At this point in my storytelling, the young teen girls gasped and then screamed, "No!"

On one day, I continued, I sat talking to my good friend Jimmy about one thing or another, and I did not hear the coach announce that today was going to be Ladies' Choice." Today, it would be the girls' turn to cross the gym and choose a partner. He went on to say—I learned later because I was not listening—that when he blew the whistle like this—*tweet*—the girls would . . .

Too late. I heard the whistle and I was off like a shot, out of my seat and running across the gym floor as fast as my chubby little legs could move me in my white-socked feet. About halfway across the floor, I realized I was the only thing moving in the gym.

"Hey," the coach yelled. "You a girl?"

At that point, I told the audience of confirmands and their parents, I stopped on the gym floor with all my classmates looking only at me. And I started to laugh, I declared. I laughed and slapped my knee and I walked back to my seat next to Jimmy, chuckling all the way, I said. And when the coach blew the whistle, I continued my telling, I sat there fearing the worst. But, you know what? I told them. Three girls walked over and asked me to dance.

And so, confirmands, I want you to learn two lessons from that story. The first lesson is: "PAY ATTENTION!" The parents chuckled. The second is no less important. The students leaned in. There will be times in your adolescence, I said, when you will do something that might embarrass you. Maybe more than once you will do such a thing. You be sure you are the first one to laugh at yourself, that you laugh the loudest and that you laugh the longest. If you learn to laugh at yourself, I promise you will have a lot more fun going through your teenage years than if you try doing everything perfectly.

On my cue, the confirmands encircled the tables and signed their names as their parents serenaded them with a silly song.

I repeated this story and this annual ceremony for a dozen years. One year, a dad sidled up to me afterward and asked in a hushed but earnest voice, "Is that really the way it happened?"

He remembered 13. He must have thought about how he would have reacted in that situation at that age, standing in the middle of the gym with all his classmates staring at him as he had just committed such an embarrassingly stupid and boneheaded move. He wanted to know, did it happen just like that.

Well, I looked him in the eye and I told him word for word exactly what I tell you now:

"Never let the truth get in the way of a good story."

I would go back to a lot of ages, but 13 would not be one of them. •

Randell Jones lives in Winston-Salem, North Carolina. He is the author of several award-winning history books, including *In the Footsteps of Daniel Boone*, and two videos. Since 2007, he has served as an invited member of the Road Scholars Speakers Bureau of the North Carolina Humanities Council. He writes, speaks, and publishes as Daniel Boone Footsteps at www.DanielBooneFootsteps.com or www.RandellJones.com.

CPSIA information can be obtained
at www.ICGtesting.com
Printed in the USA
FSHW011248140721
83104FS